Schoolboy
SCRAMBLING
and other Motorcycle Sports

Ralph Venables

 Oxford Illustrated Press Limited

For help in assembling some of the material
used in this book, the author would like to
acknowledge many persons connected with
schoolboy motorcycle sport. In particular,
the assistance given by Maurice Arden,
Bob Carpenter, Denis Davis, Bob Gollner,
Bryan Hunt, Dave Small and Keith Thorpe
was invaluable. He would also wish to
thank photographers Roy Burgess, Kerry
Dunlop, John Hopper, Bert Taunton and
Bernard Tyrer for their excellent pictures.

CONTENTS

© Oxford Illustrated Press Ltd and
Ralph Venables, 1975
Second edition 1977
Reprinted 1978
Printed and bound in Great Britain by
Butler & Tanner Ltd, Frome, Somerset

Oxford Illustrated Press Ltd,
Shelley Close, Headington, Oxford

ISBN 0 902280 28 7

Foreword by Lord Montagu

Back in the late 1950s, when land was available for motorcycle scrambles at Beaulieu, I was impressed by the enthusiasm of the younger riders whom I watched in action.

From the age of sixteen, they plunged straight into scrambling since it was what they had always wanted to do. Of course they lacked experience — simply because in those days there were no facilities for a lad aged under sixteen to participate in competitive motorcycling.

Now, happily, all that has changed. With the advent of schoolboy motorcycle sport — and its acceptance by the Auto-Cycle Union — a youngster can start competing nearly ten years earlier than he could in the era when we ran scrambles at Beaulieu.

So, by the time he celebrates his sixteenth birthday, a boy can have been building up first-hand experience of motorcycling for at least half his life. In consequence, when he enters adult sport he is already well capable of controlling fast machines.

As a character-builder, schoolboy motorcycle sport has few equals. Further, it almost compels a youngster to develop a mechanical knowledge which will be of immense value to him for the rest of his days.

In 1974, when the A.C.U. decided to give official recognition and encouragement to schoolboy motorcycling, the Youth Division was launched. Its committee was formed of parents who had already proved their ability to organise schoolboy scrambles, grass-tracks and trials.

At one of the first Youth Division committee meetings, Dick Bracher (general manager of the A.C.U.) read a letter which he had received from the Oxford Illustrated Press — asking whether there existed a book on schoolboy motorcycle sport. And, if not, would anyone care to prepare a manuscript and assemble some photographs?

Publication of a schoolboy motorcycle book was an exciting prospect, and members of the A.C.U. Youth Division committee welcomed the idea with open arms. It was something which they had long wanted.

But there was just one stumbling block. Who could write such a book? Mr. Bracher was not slow to suggest Ralph Venables, and there was not one voice raised in dissent!

A motorcycle journalist for the past forty years, Ralph Venables showed a lively interest in schoolboy motorcycle sport almost from its inception. During the intervening years, he has attended nearly a hundred schoolboy events and written literally thousands of words on the subject.

He has followed with a personal pleasure in their progress the careers of youngsters from the time they straddled their first machine to the proud day when they pitted their skill against acknowledged experts and came out on top.

Such happenings are quite commonplace now-adays, thanks solely to the opportunities provided by schoolboy sport. The ranks of tomorrow's adult champions will contain more than a smattering of former schoolboy competitors.

In this book, Ralph Venables gives the background — the full facts on what is surely the most significant happening in post-war motorcycle sport. Its progress has been nothing less than an explosion.

MONTAGU

Ralph Venables interviews Schoolboy scrambler Paul Toplis.

Introduction

Schoolboy motorcycle sport started more than fifty years ago — back in the days when a lad could obtain a driving licence at the age of fourteen.

In 1924, a London motorcycle club staged the first schoolboy trial — and this was followed a few years later by other events of a similar nature. They were ordinary tests of riding skill, with long stretches of public road linking the observed sections. High speed played no part in these contests, and it was perhaps for this reason that interest waned.

Make no mistake about it. Where motorcycle sport is concerned, the average schoolboy thinks only in terms of speed. He cares little for the finer points of balance and throttle control.

Why complicate the issue when a race has the merit of simplicity? The swiftest rider wins — and this is the straightforward set-up which appeals to every right-thinking lad. Yet it was not until 1964 that the first schoolboy scramble was held. For forty frustrating years, youngsters had been unable to get closer to the sport than watching with envy while their elder brothers or their fathers went racing.

Today there are upwards of forty schoolboy motorcycle clubs operating in Great Britain, and their number is growing all the time. Never a weekend passes without a schoolboy scramble, grass-track or trial.

Three or four clubs concentrate on trials. These events are a far cry from that first schoolboy trial of 1924. Needless to say, with entries accepted from riders as young as six, the present-day schoolboy trials are confined to private land.

There is no shadow of doubt that trials provide a good stepping-stone to scrambles or grass-track races. They develop skill and confidence — qualities which will stand a boy in good stead when he takes to the road at sixteen.

Several schoolboy motorcycle clubs have a display team — similar to the famous Royal Signals and Royal Marines 'trick riding' groups which have thrilled thousands of onlookers throughout the world. This activity, too, can provide valuable training in balance and control.

But, as soon as he is tall enough to straddle a motorcycle, today's schoolboy yearns to get racing. With luck, his father may have been a rider — perhaps a competitor — in his younger days. Should this be the case, then parental opposition is unlikely to arise.

The purchase of a machine will present problems. Financially, the choice lies anywhere between, say, £70 and £700. Before spending this sort of money, a father ought to take his son along to watch different local events. There are schoolboy motorcycle clubs in most parts of the country now, and dads should enrol their lads as members. Only in this way can they be assured of sound advice on what type of event to enter — trial, scramble, grass-track, sand-race — and what class of machine to buy or build or borrow. Every aspect should be studied carefully before reaching a decision. Some versatile youngsters compete in all four branches of the sport. But, as a general rule, it seems wise to specialise.

And it is prudent to start with a good second-hand bike, rather than pay a lot of money for a new machine which may soon be discarded if the rider's aspirations are not realised. A lad should never be forced to carry on against his wishes.

Virtually all competitive schoolboy motorcycles are of foreign manufacture — thanks to apathy and lack of foresight on the part of British factories. Yet the choice is wide. These machines are not toys. They are designed and constructed for serious competition work, with high quality components and prices to match!

With so much at stake, no hasty decisions should be made. Seek the advice of experienced riders and their fathers, try to borrow a couple of bikes for a day's trial ride — and obtain permission for somewhere to try them out.

But a boy must go carefully at first. Many lads may well be experts on the 'cycle speedway' — yet their first ride on a motorcycle can be very demoralising! A few tumbles are almost inevitable, but they all play their part in producing a safe and sensible rider.

Schoolboy motorcycle sport can be the greatest fun for all concerned. It can teach a lad to win — and to lose — without him taking the outcome too

Why complicate the issue when a race has the merit of simplicity? The swiftest rider wins — and this is the straightforward set-up which appeals to every right-thinking lad. Here, Kevin Reed sets an unbeatable pace at a Portsmouth Schoolboy Scramble.

A few tumbles are almost inevitable, but they play their part in producing a safe and sensible rider. This Ringwood Schoolboy Scramble action shot shows Adrian Tristram casting himself off while Mike Gover (40) and Keith Ree (198) pass on either side.

Shoulder to shoulder round the first bend at a charity meeting staged by the Portsmouth Schoolboy Scramble Club near Gosport. The leading riders are (left to right) Tony Tabb, Dennis Oldem, David Etheridge and Fred Miller.

The safety record appertaining to all branches of schoolboy motorcycle sport is wonderfully high. Serious accidents are almost unknown, and most of the injuries treated by the St. John Ambulance Brigade are no more than sprained ankles or wrists.

Racing on loose-surfaced sandy circuits teaches a lad to control his machine at high speed — regardless of adverse conditions. These three riders in a Ringwood schoolboy scramble are obviously well-matched.

There are few more thrilling experiences than controlling a grass-track machine in a power-slide around a slippery curve. Here, in vivid action, Richard Willis (281) and Garry May (29) fight for first place.

Mascot of Eastbourne Speedway team is Peter Johns, capable of a very stylish performance on the shale. One day, he hopes to become a speedway star, but, meanwhile, Peter is happy to compete in schoolboy grass-track races.

Every schoolboy likes to be a winner, especially when his efforts are rewarded with a laurel wreath and a silver cup. Our picture shows Garry May at the championship finals of the Kent Youth Grass-Track Riders Association.

Thousands of schoolboys dream of the day when they will be old enough to compete in motorcycle sporting events. Baby of the Waltham Chase Boys M.C.C. is John Wallace (7), shown here in thoughtful mood astride his 50cc Italjet.

seriously. It will provide the sort of mechanical knowledge which only first-hand experience can bring.

Above all, it is a pastime in which the whole family can be involved — watching, helping, encouraging, congratulating, consoling. This activity did not come into being until some seventy years after the first motorcycle was made, but it is here to stay.

Perhaps inevitably, it has its opponents and its harsh critics. Their vociferous opposition, based on ignorance, is directed at the parents who allow their sons to compete — and at the organisers who spend their weekends working so hard for absolutely no financial reward.

Yet the safety record appertaining to all branches of schoolboy sport is wonderfully high. Serious accidents are almost unknown, and official recognition by the Auto-Cycle Union (controlling body of motorcycle sport) has helped to put the whole movement on a firmer footing.

In less than a dozen years, interest has snowballed to an extent which would have been regarded as impossible by that handful of enthusiasts who formed the first schoolboy scramble club. Not far short of 4,000 youngsters participated in 1975.

No amount of antagonism can halt the onward march of schoolboy motorcycling now. Enlightenment follows slowly in its wake, and not even the most biased critics can deny the benefit which adult motorcycle sport has already derived from the existence of this training ground — a 'nursery' which may one day yield a world champion to uphold British prestige in international moto-cross.

Four minds with but a single thought! Junior competitors (all riding 50cc Suzuki machines) get away from the start of a Horsham Schoolboy Scramble Club event. The winner was David Wyatt (furthest from the camera).

Mike Lillywhite and Alan Sibley lean well to the left while rounding a fast curve at a charity schoolboy scramble near Petersfield on 8 June 1975. This was the first appearance of sidecars in a Portsmouth Schoolboy Scramble Club event.

No amount of antagonism by ill-informed critics can halt the onward march of schoolboy motorcycling now. Its popularity is growing all the time, and the entry was very large at most scrambles last season. This photograph depicts a 'full house' led by Robert West (534), Richard Bromley (130) and Noddy Attwood (34).

Fathers and sons share a common interest in schoolboy motorcycle sport. Don Schmidt points out to Dave Small some technicalities of the Mohican machines which he builds. Their younger sons — Philip Small and Martyn Schmidt — sit on the bikes, listening.

Joining a Club

To participate in any form of schoolboy motorcycle sport it is necessary that the rider shall belong to a club. There are scramble clubs, grass-track clubs and trials clubs. The majority of these come under the wing of the Auto-Cycle Union, whose Youth Division was formed in 1974. There are nearly forty schoolboy clubs affiliated to the A.C.U., and many adult clubs have junior sections.

The earliest group of clubs was the Youth Motorcycle Sporting Association, formed as far back as 1966. Today it is in fact one large club, containing a number of organisers whose area of operation stretches across the Midlands to Lincolnshire and north as far as Yorkshire.

Some of the remaining clubs have banded themselves together under the banner of the British Schoolboy Motorcycle Association, and their main interest is scrambling. From its formation in 1969, the standard of riding within the B.S.M.A. has been especially high. The clubs in this group — all based in the southern half of the country — are Corsham, Cotswold, Midland, Portsmouth, Ringwood, Severn Valley, Torbay and West Mercia.

For a while, the B.S.M.A. failed to find popularity. There was dissent within its own ranks almost from the outset, and, in an endeavour to standardise the rules, a new group was formed in early 1971. Known as the Junior Motorcycle Federation, it comprised six clubs that first year. But this number had increased to sixteen by the end of 1973, and the J.M.F. was recognised by the A.C.U. as the representative body of schoolboy motorcycle sport.

Then, with the formation of the Youth Division, every J.M.F. club affiliated to the A.C.U. in 1974 and the Federation was finally disbanded on 23 March 1975. It had written a significant chapter in the history of junior motorcycling.

Many clubs make their own insurance arrangements, some more adequately than others. Parents can take out Personal Accident cover for their sons at surprisingly low rates. Riders within the A.C.U. Youth Division enjoy the benefit of P.A. insurance available from C. T. Bowring,* at £9.00 per year for speed events, and £4.00 per year for trials. These

*C. T. Bowring; Marlowe House, Station Road, Sidcup, Kent.

premiums bring monetary compensation for various specified injuries.

The Youth Division clubs are required by the A.C.U. to take out promoters' and competitors' legal liability insurance — plus personal accident cover for officials. This amounts to £4.00 per meeting for speed events, £1.50 for trials.

World-famous riders sometimes present the awards to schoolboy motorcycle competitors. At the conclusion of a B.S.M.A. Inter-Club championship, John Giles (one of Great Britain's all-time greats in the International Six Days Trial) handed out the trophies. Here, Chris Small is receiving a handsome winged cup.

The standard of riding in British Schoolboy Motorcycle Association events has always been exceptionally high. Here is some typical action by Steven Beamish (276), Peter Archer (8), Paul Harvey (225), Pat Newman (295) and Paul Hunt (281).

Four years after receiving his first trophy at a B.S.M.A. Championship meeting, Paul Hunt had developed into one of the most stylish schoolboy scramblers in Great Britain. Here he is riding a borrowed 125cc Maico at Boxhill, Surrey, in the autumn of 1974.

At the Waltham Chase Boys Motorcycle Club annual presentation of awards in December, 1974, Geoff Chandler presented the trials championship shield to Rob Privett amid loud applause. Geoff is himself one of the most successful trials riders in England, and has given instruction to several youngsters.

Personal accident cover for competitors is not compulsory, but several brokers do in fact offer this type of insurance for schoolboys. Very reasonably, Third Party insurance is incorporated in the annual subscription for all Y.S.M.A. club members.

The Combined Insurance Co. of America* have what they call their 'Little Giant' policy, with a premium of £3.00 for six months — regardless of how many events are entered during that period. The Florida Insurance Agency,* provide personal accident cover on a somewhat different basis — 10p per rider per meeting (speed events), 5p per rider per meeting (trials).

All clubs which organise schoolboy scrambles,

The Combined Insurance Co. of America: Park House, The Broadway, London S.W.19.

The Florida Insurance Agency: 56 Norbury Road, Thornton Heath, Croydon, Surrey.

grass-tracks or sand races are acutely conscious of the need for safety precautions. The presence of trained first-aid personnel is insisted upon at every speed event.

Some clubs hold monthly meetings and social gatherings which afford an opportunity for firm friendships to be made — not only among the boys but among their families, too. Around Christmas time there are special functions where the past year's awards are presented. A successful youngster is likely to win well over 100 trophies during his eight or nine years of schoolboy sport.

World famous riders occasionally attend these Christmas parties in order to present the awards. On such occasions, a boy can truthfully boast of having received his trophy from a British champion. These are among the more blissful moments in a lad's competition career — memories which may linger for a lifetime.

A historic occasion. The first British Schoolboy Motorcycle Association Championship Scramble was held in Wiltshire on 27 September 1970. There were 120 riders, and the meeting ran so late that awards were not presented till after dark. Alongside the award winner is Bryan Hunt (later to become the first chairman of the A.C.U. Youth Division committee).

A successful youngster is likely to win well over 100 trophies during his eight or nine years of schoolboy sport. Here are Philip and Chris Small, with their proud father, displaying a selection of schoolboy scramble awards. Dave Small, himself a well-known scrambler in the 'fifties, is P.R.O. for the British Schoolboy Motorcycle Association.

Youngsters inevitably get chatting at schoolboy motorcycle sporting events, their favourite topic of conversation being the machines which they ride. Here is a typical start-line group including Alan Sibley (584), Terry Hales (19) and Wayne Blackhall (131).

Choosing a Machine

The most popular machines in schoolboy scrambles ten years ago were B.S.A. Bantams, with engine capacities of 125cc, 150cc or 175cc. But the Bantam has long gone out of production and, no matter how patriotic a parent may be, he is almost bound to buy a foreign bike for his son.

Several firms, such as Wassell, Saracen, Rickman and Cotton, market special machines with all components of British manufacture except the engines.

The 50cc Mohican has an Italian Gilera motor, and the 100cc and 125cc models are powered by German Zundapp engines. Mohican designer Don Schmidt undertakes a reed-valve conversion which adds to the cost but greatly enhances the engine's performance.

Choice of machine must be governed by two things: the type of competition for which it is required, and the amount of money which it is wished to spend.

A trials bike should be a 'plodder' — not a 'revver' — and several very suitable models are currently on the market. Best value is the 125cc four-stroke Honda, imported from Japan by Sammy Miller.* A 150cc version, specially prepared for trials, is sold at £330. But last year's most popular schoolboy trials models were the 80cc Yamaha (Japanese) at £307 and the 125cc Montesa (Spanish) at £450.

Generally speaking, a second-hand trials machine is likely to be in better condition than a grass-track or a scrambles bike — simply because it will not have been ridden at high speeds.

Many fathers attempt to adapt second-hand road machines for their sons to use in competitions. With sufficient practical experience, an ingenious parent can build a bike from scratch — designing and constructing a one-off 'special' which may in fact hold its own against production models.

Engine capacity limits are linked with the age of riders, but such restrictions vary from club to club. As a general rule, the maximum engine capacity is 250cc for trials (senior age group) and 125cc foreign or 200cc British for speed events.

In their eagerness to get started, many dads have bought — or built — machines for the use of their lads, only to find that the engines are of a greater capacity than allowed by the organising clubs. So the first step must be to decide in which type of event the boy wishes to compete — trial, scramble, grass-track or sand race. He ought then to join the nearest club which specialises in the promotion of his chosen branch of schoolboy sport, and should seek advice on the purchase of an appropriate machine.

If the decision is to start in a modest way with a second-hand bike, then there are worse places to pick up a reliable machine than at club meetings. Better to do this than to buy an unknown 'bargain' without even seeing it first.

The majority of schoolboy scramble bikes are standard production models, and these can be inspected at local motorcycle agents. The same machines are popular for grass-track and sand racing, too — but there are more 'specials' in this field.

Fortunate indeed is the boy whose father was himself a motorcycle competitor in years gone by. There is nothing to match personal experience when it comes to avoiding a bad buy.

The choice of schoolboy scramble machines currently on the market is so wide as to be bewildering. Some are good, most are foreign, all are expensive. Here are the best-known models: Aspes, Bultaco, Carabela, Cotton, C.Z., Fantic, Hodaka, Husqvarna, Italjet, Kawasaki, K.T.M., Maico, Mohican, Monark, Montesa, Malaguti, Ossa, Rickman, Suzuki, Wassell and Yamaha.

Home-built specials have always been popular, and they can cost a lot less than a production model. In the early days of schoolboy scrambling, almost any engines were used — mostly from crashed road machines.

Suzuki motors were much sought-after — 50cc, 80cc, 100cc and 125cc — also Yamaha, Zundapp, Sachs, Puch and several other two-strokes. Variety of choice has increased in recent years, and anyone with a preference for four-strokes may make good use of a Honda or a Gilera engine.

The most successful schoolboy scramble machines yet to come from Italy are the Aspes models (50cc, 100cc and 125cc). Pictured here is the 125cc version (known as the Hopi).

Only two of these neat little 'mini bikes' have been made. Designed to resemble the T.D. Jawa speedway model, they were produced by Alan Johns — one for a speedway mascot at Eastbourne, and the other for a speedway mascot in Norway. The 50cc engine is from an Ariel three-wheeler.

The Yamaha 80cc machines have proved popular with younger lads, both for scrambles and trials. Like most Japanese products, they are costly but very competitive.

A British bike designed for schoolboy scramblers is the Mohican — but it has a Zundapp motor manufactured in Germany. A reed-valve conversion to the engine is undertaken by Don Schmidt, resulting in a greatly enhanced performance.

A considerable saving can be effected by buying a trail bike instead of a pukka scrambler. Trail bikes (as distinct from trial bikes) are slanted mainly towards the American market, where the long-distance type of event — known as an enduro — created a big demand for such a motorcycle.

Without the necessity for drastic modification, these 'off road' models can be converted into really competitive machines. Total outlay could be as much as £200 less than the purchase price of a genuine moto-cross model.

Schoolboy grass-track machines are marketed by several specialist builders, such as Alf Hagon and Alan Jones. These are 'scaled down' versions of adult grass-track bikes and are very suitable for sand racing.

Right

When buying a machine, make certain that the rider can put both feet flat on the ground when he is seated astride the bike. Ten-year-old Martyn Schmidt finds this 50cc Gilera-engined Mohican plenty tall enough for his little legs.

Home-made "specials" are often used by younger riders in schoolboy trials, such as this 50cc "Bitza" ridden successfully by little Shaun Hamer in Hampshire.

It is seldom that even the most ill-fated machine is a complete write-off, but, just occasionally, the worst happens. At a Ringwood schoolboy scramble several years ago, Stephen Breaker's bike caught fire. Damage would have been negligible had fire-extinguishers been available.

With its upswept handlebars and large seat, the 125cc Bultaco looks higher than most schoolboy scramble models, but it is one of the best Spanish machines on the market. A 125cc Bultaco carried Gloucester lad Andy Bubb to many victories in last season's B.S.M.A. championship races.

A very functional machine is the 125cc C.Z. made in Czechoslovakia. It was on one of these bikes that Cambridge rider Geoffrey Mayes made his reputation as one of England's most efficient schoolboy scramblers. Geoff went on to achieve fame in adult sport.

The Swedish Monark machines imported by Meeten and Ward have 125cc Sachs engines, Motoplat transistorised ignition, Girling rear suspension and Ceriani front forks — an internationally 'mixed bag' which combines the finest components.

From Japan comes the 125cc Suzuki — a very functional machine which has set many a schoolboy on the road to success. Steven Beamish has never ridden anything but a Suzuki.

From Austria comes the 125cc K.T.M. — not yet a familiar sight in schoolboy scrambles but certainly one of the best of its kind. When they became 16 years of age, both Peter Archer and Don Harris chose 250cc K.T.M.s with which to try their luck in senior scrambling.

But the majority of fathers are prepared to construct home-made specials if it has been decided that their sons wish to go grass-track racing or sand racing. The choice of engine is wide — Honda, Suzuki, Yamaha, Puch, Ducati and even a few once familiar British motors such as Triumph and B.S.A. All are successful on the grass. There are far fewer specials seen in trials than in other branches of schoolboy motorcycle sport — simply because so many standard production machines are available.

It must be borne in mind that boys in the senior age group are permitted to ride 250cc bikes. Many such machines are on the market, 'ready to ride away' and by no means too much of a handful for any well-built lad aged twelve or thirteen.

Ideally, a youngster who has never ridden a motorcycle before, should start his competition career on a second-hand bike. Without placing too heavy a burden of responsibility on his shoulders, it will give him enormous fun. If it is a little slower and less reliable than the machines ridden by some of his friends, this could be a blessing in disguise. Motorcycle sport is a great character-builder — but a boy's personality is seldom enhanced by the belief that it is possible to buy success.

In 1974, the Suzuki really came into its own as the most popular schoolboy scramble machine on the market. Our pictures show these bikes ridden by three different competitors—in three different styles. Terry Holloway is fully at ease as both wheels sail well clear of the track, Ray Barnett likes to keep his wheels on the ground, and Chris Overd does not seem unduly worried when his bike paws the air.

Obtaining the Equipment

Regardless of whether the choice falls on a new or second-hand machine — or whether the decision is to construct a home-made 'special' out of what ever components are available — it will be necessary for the rider to be properly kitted out.

For trials, what is referred to by the Auto-Cycle Union as 'protective clothing' is not essential — but it is desirable that a boy should wear boots, gloves and helmet. Make sure that the gloves are strong without being stiff, and that the helmet is not too heavy.

For speed events, additional articles of apparel are almost a must. These include a face-mask, goggles and body-belt (a corset which supports the stomach), really tough jersey or shirt, leather or P.V.C. breeches, and perhaps knee-pads and shoulder-pads.

The most important item, for obvious reasons, is the safety helmet. This should be of an approved pattern, in sound condition and a comfortable fit. A cheap 'crash hat' is foolish economy indeed, and the price varies from around £10 to as much as £20 or even more.

Leather breeches (with built-in knee-pads) cost at least £30. So do purpose-made leather boots. Vinyl, or some other form of leather 'substitute' so popular nowadays, is quite adequate for breeches, but leather boots are essential for proper protection.

Most motorcycle agents who specialise in supplying the needs of competitors will carry a complete stock of 'gear' for riders of all ages, and it is far better to try on the clothing than to buy by post. Uncomfortable boots can be a real disaster.

Here again, personal advice from other riders (and their fathers) is invaluable. With children growing out of their boots and breeches, second-hand clothes are the answer. Again, it is imprudent to spend a small fortune on equipping youngsters who are only just getting started — they may tire of the whole project in a few weeks!

A visit to the annual Schoolboy Motorcycle Sporting Show staged by Comerfords, of Thames Ditton, Surrey, enables lads and their dads to see just exactly what clothing and equipment is available.

Bikes can be examined first-hand, components can be evaluated and discussed, clothes, helmets, boots and gloves can be tried on for comfort and size.

At this annual show, experienced schoolboy competitors are on hand to answer queries. So, of course, are members of Comerfords' staff. Films are shown, photographs are on display, names and addresses of club secretaries are available — along with membership application forms.

Alan Ward, one of the best schoolboy trials riders in the Midlands, favours no hat at all. In hot weather, a safety helmet can be very irksome — but most organisers insist on helmets being worn.

Nigel Fox, from Warsash, near Southampton, is a schoolboy scrambler who is noted for being well turned out. Only the best 'gear' is good enough for the best riders, and Nigel looks like a real professional.

Nigel Fox's machine — a 125cc Maico — is always maintained in immaculate condition. He undertakes much of the routine work himself, but, as pictured here, he leaves it to his father — a veritable wizard with the spanners — to carry out last-minute adjustments.

Chris Sutton favours a horse-riding helmet for trials — smart and light and quite satisfactory for the job in hand. But such a hat would be unsuitable for speed events.

This is a golden opportunity for newcomers to ask their questions and to gain a wealth of information on every aspect of schoolboy motorcycle sport. The show takes place each November.

One problem often overlooked is that of transport. A station waggon can accommodate a small motorcycle easily enough, but for many people it may be necessary to devise other means of taking the bike to various meetings.

A bracket for carrying the machine across the back of a car is best — if a van or open pick-up is not readily available. As a last resort, a trailer will have to be bought or built.

A good assortment of tools should also be assembled. No matter how expensive the bike may be, it will require fairly frequent adjustment — often in the short space of time between races. This is work which father and son can do together, but they can achieve little or nothing if their stock of tools is inadequate.

The brutal truth is that the cost of competing in schoolboy motorcycle sport does not begin and end with the purchase of a bike. As much as £100 can be spent on 'kitting out' a lad with first-class clothing and equipment, plus at least as much again on buying tools and a trailer.

Yet, somehow, nearly 4,000 boys competed in 1975 — at a time when most fathers were forced to tighten their belts as a result of redundancy, short-time working and all the other aspects of an economic depression.

In hundreds of families up and down the country today, schoolboy motorcycle sport is top priority. Real sacrifices are made by parents, so that their sons can compete, and the pity of it is that a father's wage-packet so seldom keeps pace with his enthusiasm!

Comerfords, of Thames Ditton, carry a complete range of schoolboy scramble equipment. Pictured here are shirt (£2.60), leather breeches (£30.00), helmet (£10.40), boots (£29.50), goggles (£2.35), gloves (£5.35), helmet-peak (£0.90), stone-guard (£2.85) and body-belt (£3.60). Not much change out of £88, but all these items of clothing are necessary in the interests of safety and comfort.

Sidecar passengers must be fully attired in protective clothing, for it is no less important to them than it is to the drivers. Kevin Thomas looks to be in full command here, with the help of passenger Mick vanLeuwen.

Full facial protection is afforded by the type of helmet favoured here by Neil Hudson, but very few such helmets are seen in schoolboy scrambles nowadays. Neil developed into an adult scrambler of outstanding ability.

The high-quality chest-protector (with shoulder-pads attached) is a Jofa product costing £10. Richard Rankcom, seen here on his 125cc Aspes at a scramble near Petersfield, is one of many riders who claim that this 'armour plating' affords considerable protection to the ribs and shoulders.

No wonder Richard Sharman (62) looked unhappy in this Ringwood schoolboy scramble of several years ago! Foolishly he was riding without goggles or gloves.

Stone-guards, such as those worn here by Norman Emery (85) and Rob Privett (103), cost £2.85. But for any boy who values his front teeth, they constitute essential equipment. Stones thrown back by spinning rear wheels can have the force of bullets!

Members of the Waltham Chase Boys Motorcycle Club have a well-trained display team which has performed at many functions throughout Hampshire. The boys look very smart in their black one-piece suits. Pictured here are John Taylor, Andy Aldous and Gary Prince — all three on one bike.

Always very neatly attired are the Imps — a boys motorcycle display team from the Adventure Holiday Project in Hackney, London. As with Waltham Chase and other display teams, the Imps are well aware that a smart appearance creates a good impression when giving public performances.

Gloves should afford a reasonable measure of protection in speed events, and those with extra padding down the backs of the fingers are best — but the padding must not be so thick as to make the gloves too stiff for comfort. Pictured here are six pairs of 'Big John' gloves (scrambles on the left, trials on the right), in front of some typical moto-cross boots and an 'Everoak' helmet.

Some of the finest boots on the market — essential items of equipment. Shown here (left to right) are the Bickers C.Z., the Comerfords Alpine and the Leask Swedish boots designed for scrambles, along with the Big John trials boot.

Riding in a Trial

Always check the bike several days beforehand — ensuring that everything is in good condition and proper adjustment. Such items as chains and control cables should be examined carefully for wear.

And always get the machine loaded into the van or pick-up (or strapped onto the trailer) the previous evening — never wait till the morning of the event.

Go to bed early, get up early, leave home with plenty of time to spare — and make sure you know just where the event is taking place. Many a trial has been lost by arriving late.

Once the venue has been reached, unload the bike and make sure that all is well. It is advisable to arrive about an hour before the start. Do not occupy this spare time by riding the bike. Much better to walk around the course, examining the layout of the observed sections and deciding on the best line around (or over) the various obstacles.

These are likely to include mud, water, deep sand, steep hills, rocks, tree-roots and other natural hazards which call for considerable skill to negotiate without penalty. High speeds are very seldom necessary.

A 'feet-up' ride through an observed section (that is to say, a non-stop ride, without either foot touching the ground) incurs no loss of marks. But penalties are imposed for footing once (one mark), twice (two marks), three or more times (three marks) and for stopping (five marks).

There is also a five-mark penalty for getting off the bike, or for riding the wrong side of a section-boundary stake, or for crossing or breaking any tape which may be used to define the lateral limits of a hazard, or for missing a section altogether.

Official observers are stationed at the sections, and they record each competitor's penalties. At the conclusion of the contest, all these scores are added up — and the winner is the rider with the lowest loss of marks.

Injury or damage seldom occur in trials, and these events form the ideal introduction to motorcycle sport. They necessitate a good sense of balance and throttle control, and help to develop the 'feel' for a machine which can be invaluable in later years.

But trials are almost bound to make the bikes muddy, and it is essential to give them a thorough clean after each event. Do this the same evening — not the next day or the day after.

Although there are only three or four boys' motorcycle clubs which specialise in trials, many adult clubs organise such events (or incorporate them within their own contests).

It is laid down by the Auto-Cycle Union that juniors and adults cannot compete for the same awards, but this rule is conveniently 'forgotten' by many clubs — a situation which often emphasises the fact that the boys can vanquish the men.

Official observers are stationed at the sections, and they record each competitor's penalties. Here, little Mark Ware is losing three marks for footing in a Ringwood schoolboy trial at Matchams Park, on the Hants-Dorset borders.

Regulations should be published beforehand for every trial, an entry form should be signed by the rider (and countersigned by a parent or guardian) and sent with the appropriate entry fee to the secretary of the meeting by a stipulated closing date.

Within a few days of the trial having taken place, efficient organisers send out detailed result sheets which indicate exactly where each competitor has lost his marks. Regardless of age, it is usual for a rider to compete as a novice (perhaps on easier sections) until he has achieved best novice performance — then he graduates to expert status.

Within the A.C.U. Youth Division, there are two country-wide championship trials each year — novice and expert. These were introduced in 1975, when the novice event was held in Hampshire and the expert event in Yorkshire.

Two or three former schoolboy trials stars, notably John Reynolds and Stephen Dudley, have already made their mark in adult competition. Many others will follow in their wake, and Chris Sutton is tipped as a future winner of the British Experts Trial.

Perfect balance and throttle-control are shown by fifteen-year-old Chris Sutton as he eases his 250cc Montesa gently over the summit of a steep hill at a Surrey Schoolboy Trials Club event. It was this sort of riding which gave Chris a 44-mark win.

Very few schoolboy scramble clubs allow girls to compete, but there is no such discrimination at the trials organised by the Waltham Chase Boys Motorcycle Club. Pictured at a trial near Chalton, Hants, are Diane Prince, Sharon Austen, Andrea Harris and Beverly Austen.

Competitors should never argue with the observers, but there is no harm in making a polite enquiry. Seen questioning his penalty with the observer and her daughter at a trial near Chichester is Chris Brooks. The 14-year-old Bognor Regis rider finished runner-up to Chris Sutton.

It is useless to ride in trials if the treads of the tyres are worn. Chris Brooks demonstrates the importance of wheelgrip as he negotiates a steeply-sloping chalk bank on his 250cc Yamaha. This is as much a test of nerves as of skill.

Richard Brooks rides a 250cc Ossa, having graduated from a 125cc Montesa. He and his cousin Chris have competed regularly in adult trials — and often lost less marks than competitors with twice their experience.

Roger Armstrong, whose father was once a successful competitor, incurs no penalty as he completes a perfect feet-up ride through this observed section in a Ringwood schoolboy trial last year.

Paul Armstrong started trials riding at the age of ten. Maybe he lacked the finesse of his elder brother, Roger, but he soon acquired a good sense of balance.

A Suzuki scrambler may not be the ideal machine for using in trials. The 50cc motor is at its best when revving hard, and this is a handicap to any rider. Sure enough, Chris Sear was often in trouble such as is pictured here — when the engine faded and the machine overbalanced.

The Waterside M.C.C. draws most of its members from schoolboys in the Southampton area, and perhaps the most stylish of these is Paul Prout. Here he has just lost a mark for footing in a Waltham Chase Boys M.C.C. trial—an event where he might have preferred not to be no. 13!

When negotiating such hazards as rocks or water, a rider achieves a lower centre of gravity by standing up (and thus transferring all his weight to the footrests). It is clear that young Andrew Arden is tackling this rocky stream in the correct manner — slow but sure.

Gordon Jackson, back to the 'fifties, was one of Britain's finest trials riders. Now a champion car trials driver, Gordon retains his interest in motorcycles, and he has provided his sons — Ross and Drew — with a 250cc Bultaco for use in schoolboy trials. Here, little Drew is seen in action on his father's farm in Kent.

Peter Stirland, five times winner of the annual Southern Experts Trial, is delighted to see his son David so keen to compete in schoolboy trials. Riding an 80cc Yamaha, David is here seen winning a Waltham Chase junior trial by a margin of more than 20 marks.

As a member of the Waltham Chase display team, Ann Doney has a good sense of balance and throttle control — something which helps her when riding in trials. Ann is pictured on her 80cc Yamaha — a little machine which suits the 11-year-old Hampshire girl perfectly.

Riding in a Scramble

Advice given at the beginning of the previous chapter is equally applicable to scrambles as it is to trials.

Indeed, a thorough inspection of the course on foot is even more to be recommended. Ample time should be allowed for this, so that the entire circuit can be examined before the commencement of practise.

For the first two or three practise laps, a rider should proceed quite slowly — familiarising himself with the course and studying the 'lines' taken by other competitors.

Then, towards the end of practise, speeds should be increased to not far short of a safe maximum. A few 'dummy runs' from the start-line are always helpful in deciding the most advantageous position on the grid.

Of obvious importance is for a rider to be ready well before the start of his race. Officials in charge of the starting area are seldom inclined to wait more than a few seconds for late-comers — and quite right too!

A good start can be crucial in any race — especially on narrow circuits where overtaking is difficult. Graham Noyce, a former schoolboy scramble champion and nowadays one of Britain's brightest hopes, asserts that a race is usually won in the first lap.

So riders must watch the starter very carefully, and be on their way just as soon as he gives the

It is very important for a rider to be ready well before the start of his race. Officials in charge of the starting area are seldom inclined to wait more than a few seconds for late-comers — and quite right too!

A good start can be crucial in any race. David Etheridge (219) pulls away from Fred Miller (32) and Dennis Oldem (93) on the first lap of a charity scramble at Stubbington, near Gosport. David went on to win, having led from start to finish.

signal. Anyone whose machine is in the wrong gear (or, worse still, in neutral) is likely to be beaten before he starts.

For the first few meetings, a boy should ride to gain experience — not to gain awards. Winning can come later, when skill and confidence have been built up to a reasonable level.

As riders begin to go faster, they will find their own limitations. They will learn not to let the front wheels slide away on slippery corners, and they will realise that leaping their machines high in the air is no way to win races.

They will find that disaster can result from landing front-wheel first after a high jump — and that violent acceleration can cause their machines to rear up and perhaps come right over backwards.

Watching other competitors is the best way to see such faults. But only personal experience will teach a lad how to correct the many errors which he is almost bound to perpetrate in his early days.

In the event of a tumble, a rider should lie still and put his arms over his head until the other bikes have gone by — then jump up and get his machine out of the way before the leaders come round on their next lap.

Practise usually commences around mid-morning, and lasts for about an hour. Duration of the actual racing varies according to daylight, but is liable to go on for as much as six hours (with an interval at half-time).

Each race seldom lasts more than a quarter of an hour, and the younger competitors have shorter races. It is customary to display a programme of races, set up on a board in the paddock, so that all riders know the sequence of events.

Entries vary from perhaps as few as fifty to as many as 200 for country-wide championship meetings, and each boy should be prepared for up to a dozen rides in one afternoon.

Most clubs divide their riders into at least four separate groups, based on age and ability (and, occasionally, on type of machine). The three main categories are Junior, Intermediate and Senior — with age as the determining factor.

A boy who starts when he is very young will spend his first three or four years in the Junior class — with a maximum engine capacity usually limited to 50cc or 80cc.

He can learn a lot in that time, and will later progress through the Intermediate and Senior categories until he has gained considerable confidence resulting from perhaps as much as ten years in schoolboy scrambling before he launches out into adult sport.

All things considered, eight years of age seems plenty young enough to start scrambling. Yet many clubs (including those in the A.C.U. Youth Division) accept entries from six-year-olds — some of whom are without question too small and timid to derive any benefit or enjoyment from participation at such a tender age.

Competitors eventually come to realise that leaping their bikes high in the air is no way to win races. Martin Randell looks surprised as his Rickman-Zundapp goes into orbit at a meeting staged by the Reading Schoolboy Scramble Club.

Disaster often results from landing front-wheel first after a high jump. The safest mode of landing is when the machine 'touches down' rear-wheel first — then there is no risk of going right on over. Graham Hardy gets his rear wheel too high at the Reading S.S.C. 10th anniversary scramble.

In the event of a tumble, a rider should lie still until the other bikes have gone by. Bill Haslam falls during the first lap of a Portsmouth Schoolboy Scramble Club race — in the path of several following machines.

Leaping through space is sometimes unavoidable if high speeds are to be maintained. Pat Rowe, from Aldershot, was inclined to overdo the 'gay abandon' during his schoolboy scrambling days — but his high jumps were usually well controlled.

Violent acceleration can cause a machine to rear up and maybe come right over backwards. Andrew Matthews got just a shade too throttle-happy at Kirdford, Sussex, and paid the price! He finished on his back — and the bike went on without him.

Peter Archer, young cousin of 1956 European moto-cross champion Les Archer, became a very confident and successful schoolboy scrambler. He was inclined to ride straight over the top of any obstacles which got in his way — such as this heap of hawthorn branches.

Thorn twigs are surprisingly tough — as Peter Archer found to his cost. He went one way, and his 125cc Suzuki went another — finishing up with its front wheel wedged in the branches of a bush. No damage — no injury.

David Thorpe, with a long succession of schoolboy scramble championship victories behind him, soon learned to take the high jumps in his stride. Here the Bracknell boy is seen above the heads of spectators at a recent Brighton scramble.

Left foot well forward as his 50cc Minarelli is cranked over for a fast left-hander, David Williams shows why he was one of the most successful junior scramblers in the south. This action shot catches little David's style perfectly.

At the height of his schoolboy scramble prowess, Jeremy Merchant was perhaps the most stylish rider in Great Britain. This quiet Dorchester lad won an immense number of trophies before moving up into adult sport.

One of the first schoolboy scramblers to be sponsored by a motorcycle dealer was the brilliant John McMillan — a championship winner in Wales as well as in England. John received support from the Windsor Comp. Shop.

One of the most methodical schoolboy scramblers in Hampshire is Chris Small. Here the Portsmouth lad is pictured keeping his 125cc Kawasaki fully under control despite a front wheel which wants to come right over backwards.

Right

Deep sandy ruts have proved the undoing of many a good schoolboy scrambler. It is all too easy to get 'cross-threaded' and lose control of the machine. Michael Webb gets his bike stuck across a rut at one of the early Ringwood meetings, and Paul Miles looks for the best way through. Many of the Ringwood circuits are sandy.

Philip Small, younger brother of Chris, was almost unbeatable when he rode in the junior age group. Now an intermediate, he is encountering stiffer opposition — but he is still winning.

Three riders — each intent on victory: Nigel Fox (237) runs wide around the outside of Kevin Clissett (75) and Gary Slight (289) at a schoolboy scramble near Gosport in 1974. Stylish Nigel went on to win — but only just.

David Thorpe (332) and Peter Archer (339) enjoyed some determined duels until Peter moved up into adult scrambling. Here they are pictured almost shoulder to shoulder — each rider wringing every ounce of speed out of his 125cc Suzuki.

The Hickstead circuit is one of the most violently undulating ever used for a schoolboy scramble. Its undulations are well revealed in this Roy Burgess action shot showing Fred Rowe (243) level with Mike Pearce (201) at a Horsham S.S.C. meeting.

Riding in Grass-Track and Sand Races

The average schoolboy grass-track circuit is 350 yards round, and anything up to eight riders take part in each race. The smoother the surface, the greater the speeds of course!

Several schoolboy grass-track riders have gone on to achieve success on the speedway after reaching the age of sixteen. Their early experience proved invaluable, and speedway promoters nowadays keep a close watch on the 'nursery' to see what talent is likely to emerge.

There are, despite the immense popularity of grass-track racing, fewer than a dozen schoolboy clubs which concentrate on this branch of the sport.

The most active are those operating in the south, but in various parts of the country are clubs which extend their scramble programme by the addition of a few grass-track meetings.

Nine clubs specialise, these being the Bristol Grass Racing Schoolboy Club, Essex Junior Grass-Track Club, Kent Youth M.C., Kent Youth G.T.R.A., Lancs Grass-Track Juniors, Midland Junior G.T.C., South-Eastern Grass-Track Juniors, South-Midland G.T.R.C., South-West Junior G.T.C.

No standard set of schoolboy grass-track rules exists, but only minor variations occur nowadays. One common factor linking the different clubs is

A battle for leadership between Guy Benfield (217) and Peter Johns (45) at the British Schoolboy Grass-Track Championships in 1974. Peter rides machines constructed by his brother Alan. Guy rides a 125cc Ducati-engined special.

Bristol lad Sean Willmott is a schoolboy grass-track rider with a rosy future. His entirely adult style and confidence have attracted wide acclaim, and he has been taken under the wing of veteran Lew Coffin. Sean's mother is secretary of the Bristol Grass-Track Schoolboy Club.

Another stylish youngster is Peter Johns, a Surrey lad whose mother is secretary of the South-Eastern Grass-Track Juniors. Peter's ambition is to follow in the footsteps of Dave Eagland or Dave Jessup — two schoolboy grass-track riders who went on to achieve fame in adult competition.

Four Lancashire riders get away from the start of a senior race, while riders for the next heat are already lined-up behind. Pictured are Arthur Lewis (88), Craig Ryding (100), Brian Chorlton (81) and Neil Collins (92). Neil is the young brother of world-famous Peter Collins.

their boundless enthusiasm for what they regard as the ultimate in schoolboy motorcycling.

Not far short of 1,000 lads between the ages of six and seventeen participated in schoolboy grass-track racing last season, many travelling great distances to compete. The standard of riding was high, and the number of accidents was low.

Much of what has been written about riding in scrambles applies to grass-track racing, though, by their very nature, the grass-track circuits are much more straightforward. Intentional 'drifting' on the bends is the aim of every competitor.

The importance of a slick start is even greater than it is in scrambles. Far fewer riders take part in any one race, and each race is of considerably less duration than in scrambling. Sheer speed is the main ingredient of success — hence the popularity of grass-track racing with the average youngster.

Schoolboy sand-racing is at present staged by only three clubs — Tees-Tyne at Redcar, Wirrall "100" at Wallasey, Auto 66 at Filey.

The Tees-Tyne M.C.S.R.C. has featured school-boy races in most of its sand-race meetings since the summer of 1973. Three schoolboy races are included in each Tees-Tyne meeting.

Most schoolboy sand-race circuits are about 600 yards in length, allowing for more prolonged high speeds than in grass-track racing. Machines used on the sand are basically similar to those ridden in scrambles or on the grass — although gear ratios should be higher.

Sand-race circuits are often wet, and ignition systems must be shielded against water. An efficient air-cleaner is even more desirable on the sand than elsewhere.

But no amount of protection will entirely exclude the grit, and to guard against corrosion by salt water (ruinous to some metals) machines must be thoroughly hosed down after every meeting.

For youngsters who yearn to go road-racing, immense enjoyment can be derived from competing in sand-race events. They come closer to the "real thing" than grass-tracks, and several schoolboy sand exponents have become top-class road racers in later years.

The technique for grass-track and sand-racing is essentially different from that adopted when scrambling. The machines should be broad-sided round the bends. 'Power sliding' is far less appropriate on the rough surfaces encountered at scrambles.

Speeds are higher on the long sand-race circuits, yet, mainly on account of their width, these courses provide what is recognised as the safest form of motorcycle racing.

The skill of a rider — rather than the flat-out speed of his machine — counts for less on the sand than in scrambles. From a competitor's point of view, therefore, sand-racing may bring less satisfaction. And the scarcity of suitable venues will always keep it a minority sport.

But it has a happy atmosphere, and has changed little since the great days of Pendine, Saltburn and other half-forgotten pre-war meetings. Last season's racing ran from 16 February to 23 November.

There is plenty of action at the Lancashire meetings, as typified by this shot of Keith Rylance (201) and Terry Beckett (96) at last year's third L.G.T.J.R. championship event.

One of the best-known competitors in Great Britain is Peter Collins. His young brother Neil has his sights on similar success, and he rides a 125cc Honda in Lancashire Grass Track Junior events. Here he is seen cutting inside David Lilley (100 Yamaha).

The mud flies high as fearless Bobby Garrad power-slides round the circuit at a South-Eastern Grass-Track Juniors meeting in Kent. During the first few events last season, many tracks were almost too wet to use — then the weather changed abruptly and the main problem was dust.

Determination written in every line, 13-year-old Kevin May achieved many successes in Kent Youth Grass-Track meetings. He is seen here at the Championship finals, riding a 200cc Triumph with all the assurance of a veteran.

Tony Snook, riding a very stark 200cc Triumph Tiger Cub, is seen out on his own at this British Schoolboys Championship meeting in Kent. These Cub engines are in short supply now, and most schoolboy grass-track machines have foreign motors.

Winning four of his five races at the 1974 Kent Youth Grass-Track Riders Association championship finals, Swansea rider Charlie Huxtable was one of the most successful competitors at that meeting. The Welsh lad has now moved up among the men, riding a 350cc Godden Jap.

Two of the most dedicated grass-track riders are Sean Willmott (Bristol) and Pip Lamb (Hereford), a couple of West Country schoolboys who have enjoyed many fine battles. Here they are pictured, shoulder to shoulder, with Sean trying to get by on the outside.

In their last season as schoolboy competitors, Charles Nixon (101) leads Chris Morriss (107) and David Moore (103) in a race for 16-year-olds at a Lancashire meeting last May.

At a British Schoolboy Grass-Track Championship near Brenzett, Kent, this photograph gives a good idea of the determination shown by most competitors on important occasions such as these. Martin Aylward (261) narrowly leads Keith May, Kevin Brice and Alan Saunders.

A swift start is vital in grass-track events, where races are seldom of more than four laps. Andrew McEwen (112) and Carl Clarke (142) seem still to be fighting for wheelgrip at the start of this Lancashire meeting, while Chris Morriss (107) gets so much traction that his front wheel lifts. On the right, Terry Rawlinson (171) helps forward movement with some determined footwork.

In 1974, Martin Dixon won the Class B Championship at the Tees-Tyne schoolboy sand races, and was in consequence up-graded to Class A for 1975. He is pictured at Redcar, Yorks, on his 125cc Wassell.

Knowing the Rules

Since the earliest days of schoolboy motorcycle sport, different clubs have had different rules. Many unsuccessful endeavours were made to standardise the regulations, and now there is at last some measure of uniformity between the various groups.

Even so, several basic differences still persist — the most troublesome being those relating to minimum and maximum ages, and to minimum and maximum engine capacities.

More than one attempt was made to set a maximum price of machines, in an effort to stem the rapid 'inflation' which literally forced hundreds of families out of the sport. A figure of £100 was fixed as applicable — but the idea never caught on.

So, today, the only limit is in engine capacity — not in price. But, even here, there is divergence from group to group. As a general rule, the maximum for trials is 250cc, and the maximum for speed events is 125cc foreign and 200cc British.

Anyone becoming involved in schoolboy motorcycle sport would be foolish not to familiarise himself with regulations. For a youngster not yet into his teens, such things are likely to be tedious and tiresome, but, for the sake of his son, every father should have a working knowledge of what is allowed.

The rules under which different groups operate are listed at the back of this book. At first glance they may appear long-winded and over-complex, but they have been arrived at by a long process of elimination on the part of those officials whose responsibility it is to supervise the meetings.

A good clerk of the course never allows his club's rules to be broken — for they have been compiled mainly in the interests of safety and fair play. Parents who try to 'bend' the regulations are in reality doing their sons a disservice.

The Auto-Cycle Union has its own rules applicable to every branch of adult motorcycle sport. Under the title: 'Standing Regulations' they are published in the annual A.C.U. Handbook. These rules apply to Youth Division events except where varied by the following regulations drawn up specifically for schoolboy events.

1. ORGANISING PERMITS. An application for Permit to organise a competition shall be made on the appropriate form and sent to ACU headquarters. Competitions may be Closed to Club (restricted to members of the organising club), Restricted (restricted to members of clubs in an ACU Local Centre or Youth Division Region) or National (open to members of all clubs affiliated to the ACU).

Youth Division National Championship events shall be allocated by the Youth Division Committee.

Permit Fees, if any, shall be decided by the Youth Division Committee.

2. JOINT ADULT/YOUTH EVENTS. Youth Classes may be included in adult events of Closed to Club and Centre Restricted status. In the case of Speed Events the practising and racing for the Youth Classes must be run separately from the Adult Classes and the age groups also separated. In trials, it is considered unnecessary to separate Youth and Adult classes but they must compete for separate awards.

Adult Clubs promoting competitions including both adult and youth classes shall organise these under the normal adult permit issued by the local Centre. The Youth Division Regulations, however, shall apply to all youths taking part in these competitions.

3. TEMPORARY COURSE CERTIFICATES (SPEED EVENTS). A Temporary Course Certificate is not required for a youth event to which the general public is not admitted.

4. INSURANCE. The ACU lays down minimum insurance requirements and provides policies to implement these. Insurance cover for Promoters' and Competitors' Legal Liability, Personal Accident to Officials and Landowner's Idemnity is obligatory. Cover for Personal Accident to Drivers is optional but is available from the ACU insurers to whom direct application should be made.

The Organising Permit not only authorises the promotion of the competition but is also the Insurance Cover Note for the event. The Insurance premiums are payable with the Permit Fee on application for a Permit.

In 1973, Fred Rowe (243) realised the possibilities of overtaking a slower rider round the outside of a bend. Here 'Fearless Fred' is seen at Chiddingfold, Surrey, about to pass Paul Hunt (281).

By 1974, casting discretion to the winds, Fred Rowe was inclined to overdo the use of corners as a passing place. Our photograph depicts Fred broadsiding into the chalk rocks at Butser after overtaking Peter Archer at what proved too great a speed.

Left
Kevin Reed has developed into one of the Horsham Schoolboy Scramble Club's most forceful riders. Here he gives his Suzuki a big handful of twist-grip as he power-slides round a left-hander.

Right
Another neat Horsham S.S.C. member is Tony Verbeeten, never afraid to keep the throttle open — even in the bumpy and dusty conditions depicted in this Roy Burgess photograph.

Below
Tapes, not ropes, are used for setting out the circuit at most schoolboy scrambles — simply because a rider can suffer a real 'burn' if he catches his neck on a rope at high speed. This picture shows David Thorpe setting a hot pace.

Considerable sums of money have been raised for charity by the efforts of schoolboy motorcycle clubs. This photograph was taken at a Portsmouth S.S.C. charity meeting, and it shows Richard Sharman (62), Marcus Laurent (6), Russell Lockyer (2) and Kevin Reed (311). Well silenced machines are a 'must' when racing in close proximity to houses, as seen here.

5. COMPETITION LICENCES. Competition Licences are not required for youth competitions.

6. RESPONSIBILITY FOR YOUTH ENTRANTS. The parent, guardian, or responsible adult must accompany a Youth Entrant to a meeting and stay for the duration of the time that the youth is present.

7. PROTESTS. A Protest may be made by a parent, guardian, or responsible adult on behalf of a youth competitor and the parent, guardian or responsible adult may represent the youth at all subsequent proceedings.

8. COMMERCIAL SPONSORSHIP. Commercial advertising connected with youth entrants or youth competitions shall not be permitted unless authorised by the Youth Division Committee.

9. OFFICIALS. The officials responsible for the supervision of a competition are the Stewards of the Meeting. At a Closed to Club meeting the number of Stewards shall be from one to five and shall be nominated by the promoting club. At a Restricted

meeting the number of Stewards shall be from two two five and shall be nominated by the promoting club. At a National meeting there shall be from three to five Stewards at the meeting at least one of whom shall be nominated by the Youth Division Committee.

10. ACCEPTANCE OR REFUSAL OF ENTRY. Drivers whose entries are not accepted must be notified as soon as possible.

11. CHANGE OF MACHINE. A change of machine may be permitted provided that prior notification is made to the Clerk of the Course before the event in which the change is to take place. The same machine must be used throughout any one event, i.e. both in the the heat and final.

12. JURISDICTION. Youth members of Clubs affiliated to the ACU or ACU Youth Division may take part in competitions promoted by Clubs or organisations not affiliated to the ACU. This dispensation in respect of GCR No. 6 may be withdrawn, partially or completely, at any time at the discretion of the Management Committee.

Some clubs stipulate that riders should keep their left hands on their helmets immediately prior to the start of a race. This prevents riders from holding their clutch lever out — thus making it impossible for a machine to be in gear and the start to be 'jumped.' In this picture, Clive Collins (3) indicates that he is not ready to start.

13. AGE GROUPS. A youth may opt to transfer to adult competitions on or after his sixteenth birthday but having once competed as an adult he may not revert to youth competitions except in Trials.

When a youth reaches the maximum age limit for his group he may, if he so wishes, continue to compete in that group until the end of the calendar year except that he may not continue beyond his 17th birthday.

No youth may compete before the 6th birthday nor after the 17th birthday.

Within these limits, youths will compete during the 1978 season in classes determined by date of birth as given below, where all dates and approximate ages are inclusive.

Moto Cross (Scrambles), Sand Racing and Trials: Class D (Cadets) — born between 1 Jan. 1970 to 31 Dec. 1971 (approx. ages 6 to 7). Class C (Juniors) — born between 1 Jan. 1967 to 31 Dec. 1969 (approx. ages 8 to 10). Class B (Intermediates) — born between 1 Jan. 1964 to 31 Dec. 1966 (approx. ages 11 to 13). Class A (Seniors) — born between 1 Jan. 1961 to 31 Dec. 1963 (approx. ages 14 to 16).

Grass Track Racing: Class D (Cadets) — born between 1 Jan. 1970 and 31 Dec. 1971 (approx. ages 6 to 7). Class C (Juniors) — born between 1 Jan.

1967 and 31 Dec. 1969 (approx. ages 8 to 10). Class B (Intermediates) — born between 1 Jan. 1965 and 31 Dec. 1966 (approx. ages 11 to 12). Class A (Seniors) — born between 1 Jan. 1963 and 31 Dec. 1964 (approx. ages 13 to 14). Class A1 (Seniors) — born between 1 Jan. 1961 and 31 Dec. 1962 (approx. ages 15 to 16).

14. ENGINE CAPACITY CLASSES. The maximum engine capacity permitted for machines used in the Age Groups set out in Regulations No. 13 are as follows:

Moto Cross (Scrambles) and Sand Racing: Class D: Maximum 50cc. Class C: Maximum 80cc. Class B: Maximum 100cc (foreign); 150cc (British). Class A: Maximum 125cc (foreign); 200cc (British).

Trials: Class D: Maximum 80cc. Class C: Maximum 100cc. Class B: Maximum 200cc. Class A: Maximum 250cc.

Grass Track Racing: Class D: Maximum 50cc. Class C: Maximum 100cc. Class B: Maximum 150cc. Class A: Maximum 200cc. Class A1: Maximum 250cc.

15. NUMBER PLATES. In Speed Events the number plates shall be coloured as follows:

Class D: White plates with Black numbers. Class C: Black plates with White numbers. Class B:

Green plates with White numbers. Class A: Blue plates with White numbers. Class A1: Yellow plates with Black numbers.

Where yellow, green or blue are required the colours shall comply with BS4805:1972 as follows: Yellow 10E53; Green 14E53; Blue 18E53.

16. UPGRADING. A driver may be upgraded into a higher group before reaching the age normally required subject to the agreement of the driver's parent or guardian and the Youth Division Committee which may delegate its authority in this matter to a Sub-Committee.

17. SAFETY PRECAUTIONS (SPEED EVENTS). The ACU 'Requirements for Safety Precautions at all Speed Events' shall be complied with at all events to which the general public is admitted.

At events where the general public is not admitted the requirements for 'double roping' may be relaxed provided that where spectators are permitted to foregather adequate running off space and single roping is provided and the appropriate Prohibition Notices displayed.

Courses shall be marked in such a manner that no danger is presented to the drivers.

At all Speed Events First Aid personnel must be in attendance.

18. CHAIN GUARDS. A chain guard or guards must be fitted on all machines to cover the entry of the chain to the gear box and rear sprockets.

19. WHEELS. Disc or wire-spoked wheels only are permitted on machines in speed events. Bladed wheels are not permitted.

20. CONTROL OF EXHAUST NOISE. The Clerk of the Course may exclude any machine which he considers excessively noisy.

Random checks by official ACU operators using ACU approved noise meters may be made of the noise level of any motorcycle taking part in any meeting.

A driver who fails to comply with the requirements of this regulation shall be excluded.

The noise level of a motorcycle must not exceed 110 dBA. The method and conditions for the measurement of noise emitted by a motorcycle shall be the official FIM test as follows:

The microphone shall be placed 0.5 m from each exhaust pipe outlet at an angle of 45° from the rear

of the centre line of the motorcycle and at least 0.2 m above the ground. The mean piston speed for the test shall be 13 m/sec.

Any form of silencing must be visible and permanently attached to the exhaust system of the machine.

21. HELMETS. Speed events: Helmets bearing the ACU stamp and in sound condition and properly fitted must be worn by all drivers while practising and racing. Only helmets providing full protection to the temples will be permitted.

Trials: Helmets bearing the ACU approved stamp or helmets of a B.S.I. approved type for road use must be worn by all drivers in all trials.

22. PROTECTIVE CLOTHING. Speed events: Protective clothing consisting of leather breeches (or breeches made of an ACU-approved substitute material, but not nylon), gloves, knee-length leather boots and a leather jacket or a long-sleeved jersey bearing the ACU stamp must be worn by all drivers in speed events.

Nothing hard such as money or tools may be carried in the pockets at any time.

23. GOGGLES. Speed events: It is recommended that goggles are worn at all times when conditions are suitable.

Goggles (and spectacles if worn) shall be of non-splinterable material.

24. FALSE START (SPEED EVENTS). A driver who causes two false starts may be excluded from the race.

It is emphasised that the above regulations, applicable to A.C.U. Youth Division events only, are supplementary to the A.C.U. General Competition Rules and the various Standing Regulations for each type of competition.

Different schoolboy motorcycle clubs have their own regulations, and a selection of these will be found on pages 77-86. If there is any doubt, copies of the appropriate rules should be obtained from the club secretaries whose names and addresses are listed after the club rules.

Information relating to the Auto-Cycle Union (with particular reference to the Youth Division) is available from the A.C.U., 31 Belgrave Square, London, SW1X 8QQ.

History of Schoolboy Scrambling

Although, as mentioned in the Introduction, schoolboy motorcycle sport started with trials, it was not until schoolboy scrambling was introduced — in 1964 — that any real impact was made.

Adult scrambling goes back to the spring of 1924, when a group of enthusiastic clubmen in Camberley, Surrey, decided to stage a hitherto untried type of sport — cross-country motorcycle racing.

Known as the Southern Scott Scramble, this was the first event of its kind anywhere in the world. True, in 1923 there had been so-called Rough Riders Rambles on the rugged Lancashire moors, but these were not competitions.

It was on 29 March 1924, that history was made — at Frimley, Surrey. Some eighty riders started in that first Southern Scott Scramble, and barely half the entry completed the full distance.

Scrambling was here to stay, and literally thousands of events have been held during the past fifty odd years. Under the name Moto-Cross, it became popular on the Continent in the late 'forties, and today there are few countries where this branch of motorcycle sport is not familiar.

Surprising, therefore, that nobody got around to organising a schoolboy scramble for forty years after that first 'Southern Scott' had set the scene. But it was not until October, 1964, that Denis Davis sowed the seed which was soon to grow into perhaps the most remarkable development that motorcycle sport has witnessed.

At Goring Heath, near Reading, Mr. Davis laid out an unpretentious little track for the benefit of his son Keith and two kindred spirits — Robert Vickers and Graham Butler.

From that humble beginning, schoolboy scrambling escalated in a way which nearly swept the early organisers off their feet. Exactly a year later, the first schoolboy championship scramble was held — at Woodcote, Berks. The winner was Barry Sykes.

By that time, Denis Davis had founded the Reading Schoolboy Scramble Club. Its success, and the publicity accorded to its first championship meeting, encouraged other enthusiasts to form similar clubs up and down the country.

In May 1966, Ken Jepson staged his inaugural event at Droitwich, Worcs, under the banner of the Hanbury S.S.C. Soon, Roy Grainger formed a club at Corsham, Wilts, and then Dave Poole did likewise at Ringwood, Hants.

Under the enthusiastic guidance of Rita Weston, a Horsham club came into being in 1969, and in October of that year the first Inter-Club Championship was held near Banbury, Oxon. A month later, the British Schoolboy Motorcycle Association was formed.

The Youth Motorcycle Sporting Association had already been set up, in 1966, at the suggestion of

One of the most dashing riders ever to emerge from the Ringwood Schoolboy Scramble Club was Trevor Hardiman (78), here seen leading Martin Cook. Many championship trophies found their way onto the Hardiman sideboard.

Winner of the first All-Britain Schoolboy Championship (senior category), held near Coventry, was Graham Noyce — later to become one of Great Britain's most promising scramblers after serving his apprenticeship with the Rickman brothers at New Milton, Hants.

Ken Jepson and Roy Grainger. Operating mainly in the East Midlands, the Y.M.S.A. is nowadays responsible for the organisation of many excellent events. They have a choice of nine venues, with a different organiser for almost every one.

With no controlling body to ensure standardisation of rules, the ever-growing number of schoolboy motorcycle clubs operated under various different regulations — something which inevitably gave rise to problems at national championship meetings.

But despite these difficulties, schoolboy scrambling flourished. Soon, clubs were formed in Wales, then Scotland, then Ireland. Many adult clubs, perhaps with an eye to future membership, set up junior sections which catered for lads too young to ride on the road. These clubs concentrated mainly on trials.

Scrambling is the roughest and toughest form of motorcycle sport — with most of the circuits set out on undulating terrain where mud and sand and stones are by no means the only hazards encountered. True, some of the courses are fairly smooth, but such circuits provide little idea of what a lad must expect when he moves up into adult sport.

Back in the autumn of 1966, schoolboy sidecar scrambling was introduced by the Y.M.S.A., but after two or three meetings it was decided to drop this class. Support was poor, and parents felt that the danger was too great. But sidecars were revived by the Portsmouth S.S.C. nine years later, this time with more success.

The first schoolboy club for grass-track enthusiasts was formed in January 1967. Known as the Kent Juniors, their opening event took place on 2 April at Bredhurst, and among the winners were Dave Jessup, Dave Kennett and Gary Keown — names which nowadays are familiar to all followers of speedway racing.

Similarly, many schoolboy scramblers have become well-known in adult moto-cross. Such riders as Graham Noyce, Chris Clark, Neil Hudson and literally dozens more of today's top riders started competing before they were in their teens.

For the 'feet-up' devotees, Keith Dopson launched the Surrey Schoolboy Trials Club in March, 1972. Eight months later, the Waltham Chase Boys Motorcycle Club was formed — and from the ranks of these two clubs have already come several brilliant adult riders.

There is no questioning the fact that schoolboy motorcycle sport must eventually prove to be the cradle from which will emerge world champions. And that time may be very near at hand.

Several films have already been made (one for television) with schoolboy scrambling as their theme. They went some way towards enlightening members of the general public, but ignorance is still the main basis for most criticism.

Literally millions of people in this country have no

A reminiscent picture of Chris Small, aged eleven, holding a precarious advantage over two rivals at a Ringwood Schoolboy Scramble Club meeting. In those days, Chris rode a Whitlock-framed Suzuki.

idea that any form of organised schoolboy motorcycle sport exists. Others are vaguely aware that there is such a thing — but they are apt to look down upon it as being no more than little children playing with expensive toys.

Gradually, perhaps, a better understanding will come — a wider acceptance of the fact that schoolboy motorcycle sport is a very worthwhile pastime.

The 'image' of schoolboy scrambling has been much enhanced by several charity meetings, the most successful of which was staged at Foxham, near Chippenham, last May — when no less than £850 was raised for the local St. John Ambulance Brigade.

Right
Ian Ruddick sails stylishly over the crest of a steep bank while competing in a Horsham Schoolboy Scramble Club event at Halnaker chalk pit, near Chichester. This was the fifth schoolboy scramble club to be formed.

Below
Weavers Down, near Liphook, Hants, was one of the best scramble circuits in the south. But there were complaints about noisy machines, so permission to use the land was withdrawn last year. Our photo is typical of the close racing seen at this venue.

One of the most popular scramble circuits in England is that situated at Golding Barn, near Brighton. Steven Beamish did much of his riding there — for the track is only a few hundred yards from his home. Steven became an expert within the first six months of moving up from the boys to the men.

Horsham Schoolboy Scramble Club champion, Chris Clark made rapid strides through the novice ranks when he became sixteen. Later he went to work for Brian Leask, importer of Husqvarna and Yamaha machines (and himself a former scrambles rider of great ability).

A strong and determined lad is David Etheridge, who spent two successful seasons as a schoolboy scrambler in England before returning to Australia. David rode the first 125cc Yamaha to be seen in British scrambles.

Perry Leask, son of Brian Leask, is developing into one of the best schoolboy scramblers in Sussex. As he corners rapidly on his Yamaha, he takes a cool glance at the brave man who is taking his photograph.

Mike Pearce (201), Pat Rowe (242), Richard Morgan (248) and Kim Hardy (227) all made a name for themselves in adult sport within a few months of moving out of schoolboy scrambling.

Machine Preparation and Maintenance

Careful maintenance of any competition motor-cycle is a 'must' if troubles are to be avoided. Indeed, it can play a significant part in the rider's success.

If components are properly adjusted and in good working order, the machine is likely to give its 'jockey' an effortless ride. If nothing is right, he is destined to have a hard struggle.

From a financial point of view, money spent on replacement of faulty parts will keep a bike in competitive trim for many years. Without regular maintenance, 'decay' will soon set in — and this could mean buying a new bike far too frequently.

Even a brand new model should be checked carefully, paying particular attention to getting the controls well positioned so that everything 'comes to hand' and operates easily.

It is essential that, when seated normally, a rider's feet should reach the ground — and that the handlebars are neither too high nor too low.

If both feet cannot be planted firmly on the ground when the rider is sitting astride the machine, then some of the sponge rubber should be removed from inside the seat (and the seat recovered by a professional upholsterer).

Shape and size of handlebars can be critical. There is an almost unlimited selection on the market, and it is much wiser to buy new bars than attempt any drastic modification of the old ones.

When a rider obtains a second-hand machine, it may well be that the bike has already been overhauled and all faulty parts renewed. Even so, common sense should persuade a new owner to make a thorough check. Better sure than sorry.

A careful examination of the cylinder bore and the piston rings is something not to be shirked. Check the small-end bearing — and the big-end bearing, also. If there is any play, both should be renewed. It is false economy to make do with worn bearings.

Crankcase oil seals, too, must be in perfect condition if trouble is to be avoided. Replacement of these seals is a job not to be attempted without reference to a workshop manual. The correct ignition settings can also be obtained from this source.

Regular servicing of a competition motorcycle is essential, and there are certain items which must be inspected after every meeting — especially if the course has been a wet one.

Top priority is to keep the bike clean. Freedom from dirt and rust is vital, for it simplifies detection of cracks in the frame, handlebars, mudguards, exhaust system, and so on.

At the finish of a muddy meeting, try to remove most of the dirt before setting off for home. But be careful not to leave heaps of mud on the road or at the entrance to someone's front drive. Not everybody is a motorcycle enthusiast!

A thorough hosing-down may seem too drastic, but a muddy machine is no credit to its rider — and maintenance cannot be carried out properly unless everything is clean. Even so, avoid over-enthusiastic use of a pressure hose. The worst enemies of any competition bike are mud and water, and indiscriminate hosing can do more harm than good.

The entry of dust and sand into the engine (by way of the carburetter) can do untold damage, and this must be guarded against by a really efficient air-filter. Two basic varieties are available. One is the dry paper type — which should be removed and 'blown out' with an air-hose after every meeting. Renew the paper element as soon as it starts to tear or has become wet.

The other is the oil-impregnated 'foam' type — which should be removed and cleaned in petrol, then washed in warm water and detergent before rinsing in clear water. When dry, the element should be soaked in a petrol-oil mixture, squeezed out and allowed to dry a little before refitting.

It is prudent to coat the inside of the filter chamber (and inlet tract between air filter and carburetter) with grease. This helps to catch any stray particles of dust and grit, and if a lot of dust is found in the inlet tract then something is wrong — either with the element itself or with the fitting of the filter box.

Various plastic caps are available for fitting over carburetters, to prevent the ingress of water by way of the throttle cable or screw-top adjuster. Even with these caps fitted, carburetters should be dismantled and cleaned regularly.

Father advises son. Robin Doney tells his son Robert to check every nut and bolt for tightness. Vibration can loosen a nut in a surprisingly short space of time.

Cousin advises cousin. Young Paul Doney tells cousin Rob to check the bolts holding down the cylinder head of his 150cc Honda. Slack head-bolts can cause 'blown' gaskets.

Prevention of water shorting out the ignition system can be ensured in several ways. A waterproof cap over the spark-plug is invaluable, and the other end of the high-tension lead should be sealed with plasticine.

Any machine which has a contact-breaker points cover may benefit from the appication of plasticine around the cover — but this should be removed after each meeting (otherwise the air-tight seal could cause condensation in the contact-breaker).

Ignition, even on today's most sophisticated machines, can be disconcertingly temperamental, and every component must be maintained in tip-top condition. In particular, 'pitted' contact-breaker points should be renewed to avoid misfiring and poor starting.

Spark-plugs need a thorough cleaning (sand-blasting is best) after every meeting. Gaps should be checked carefully, and it is essential to ensure that the high-tension lead is making good contact with the plug. The entire ignition system should be coated externally with a spray-on damp resistent.

Control cables must be examined for damage. At least once a month, dismantle the cables and check for fraying of the inner strands. Then lubricate with a very light oil, replace the cables and tape around the tops (to stop dirt getting in, and the cables jumping out).

The throttle twistgrip assembly should be cleaned and lightly lubricated from time to time, likewise the handlebar levers. Protective covers for these levers are available, and they certainly help to exclude mud and water.

The levers themselves should be examined for possible cracks. It is advisable to refrain from having the levers so tight on the handlebars that they are absolutely immovable. If rigidly affixed, in the event of a tumble the levers may snap off instead of turning harmlessly. But they must be tight enough to avoid dropping.

The frame should be inspected carefully for cracks, likewise footrests, brake mechanism, suspension units and head stock. Check steering head by applying front brake and rocking machine backwards and forwards to reveal any movement in head bearings.

Chains must be taken off and cleaned after every meeting, for they are costly items which can have only a short life if not looked after properly.

Grit and grime should be removed with a wire brush, then the chains soaked in petrol and boiled in 'Linklife' or 'Chainguard' or similar graphite grease (which becomes very thin when hot — then sets into a protective covering when cold).

Remove both wheels once a month, completely dismantle brakes and clean. Shoes should be brushed, and, if necessary, 'roughed up' with a coarse file if the linings have become polished. Drums should be wiped out, and rubbed lightly with very fine emery-paper. Make sure that the operating

Modern motorcycles can survive a lot of hammering at high speeds on rough ground, but a rear chain adjusted too tight is likely to snap as a result of heavy landings after a jump. This is what happened to David Wyatt at a scramble near Chichester, where the broken chain was the only thing which stopped him winning all his races.

When climbing steep slopes, a machine must not falter. If the engine is worn, the carburetter badly adjusted or the jet choked, if the sparking plug is dirty or the ignition system past its prime, then the rider will be suffering under a severe handicap. Chris Brooks is careful to keep his bike in perfect condition always.

When a boy is old enough to ride a motorcycle, he is old enough to carry out routine maintenance. Paul Doney has considerable skill in the use of tools, and he hopes to join his father in the garage business when he becomes 16.

It is at moments like this when a well-maintained machine gives a comforting sense of confidence to any competitor. Stephen Walker is seen rounding the last bend in a race at Golding Barn, Sussex, with the throttle wide open and everything working just as it should.

Bob West (534) and Richard Bromley (130) are schoolboy scramblers whose bikes are always kept in good adjustment. They see no need to be burdened with unreliable machinery.

arms rotate freely in the brake plates.

Inspect spokes, and tighten if any are loose. When the wheels are back in place, be careful to adjust rear chain to correct tension — and check that the chain guide is not out of line. A guide which has been knocked sideways can cause the chain to come adrift.

Remember — a chain (especially when brand new) may well need further adjustment after the machine has covered a few miles. Never allow it to run too slack. And, just as important, never adjust it too tight.

Examine front and rear sprockets regularly, and check the security of rear sprocket bolts. From time to time, remove and examine rear suspension units, and ensure that the swinging arm has not developed any side-play. Operation of the rear dampers must be just right, if the bike is to handle well at speed.

Front fork efficiency, too, is important. Drain the forks and replenish with the correct amount of oil. In warm weather, a thicker oil can be used. And on the subject of oil, the gearbox should be drained and refilled several times each season.

Every few weeks, knock out wheel bearings, wash in petrol and apply hub-grease. A liberal smearing of grease will go a long way towards keeping mud and water out of the bearings.

Examine tyres for any bad cuts, and ensure that there has been no 'creep' of the tube within the cover. Most rear tyres with square block tread can be changed around the other way if the front edge of the blocks shows signs of wear. Such a change will prolong the useful life of any cover.

Once every two or three months, remove and inspect the fuel tank for possible damage (either as a result of a tumble, or of chafing against the top frame tube). A leaking petrol tank can be unpleasant — and dangerous.

Check all nuts and bolts for tightness — and pay particular heed to the exhaust system. Heat and vibration are inclined to cause cracks in the bracket securing areas, and many races have been lost as a result of exhaust pipes breaking loose.

Most machines do have their weak points. Experience will tell what to look for — and what spare components are likely to be needed at a meeting. But the modern motorcycle is well on the way to being a masterpiece of engineering, and, if maintained properly, will give years of good service.

Newcomers to schoolboy sport should not hesitate to seek advice. Far better to get personal instruction than to do a job by trial and error — perhaps with costly consequences . . .

Extracts from Typical Club Rules

TORBAY SCHOOLBOY SCRAMBLE CLUB

Machine Regulations:

1. Frames may be of any type passed as safe by the scrutineer.

2. Handlebar levers must have permanent metal ball ends.

3. Footrests must be secure and safe.

4. Edges and ends of frames, mudguards, footrests and all other parts must be blunt and unlikely to cut.

Clive Dopson's father organises schoolboy trials in the Home Counties. Regulations are strictly enforced, but they are simple and sensible — and accepted in a good spirit by all competitors in Surrey Schoolboy Trials Club events. Here is Clive, competing in one of his father's trials.

5. Throttles must be self-closing and stop engine when shut.

6. Tyres may be of any type except a ribbed tread pattern.

7. Brakes must be efficient and have independent operation on each wheel.

8. Silencers must be efficient and securely attached.

9. Chain guards must be fitted on primary chains, giving complete enclosure.

10. Wheel sizes are optional, but rider must be able to touch the ground with both feet when seated astride the machine.

11. Fuel is restricted to commonly available pump petrol, and the use of methanol or any other "dope" is not permitted.

12. Sponsored machines shall not be used at any meeting if ridden for gain or reward.

Age Groups:

Class A — 14 to 16 years inclusive. British engines up to 200cc, foreign engines up to 125cc (reboring up to +060" permitted). Larger foreign engines reduced in capacity not acceptable. Numbers: white figures on blue background.

Class B — 11 to 13 years inclusive. British engines up to 125cc, foreign engines up to 100cc (reboring up to +060" permitted). Larger foreign engines reduced in capacity not acceptable. Numbers: white figures on blue background.

Class C — 6 to 10 years inclusive. British engines up to 100cc, foreign engines up to 50cc. (reboring up to +060" permitted). Larger foreign engines reduced in capacity not acceptable. Numbers: white figures on black background.

YOUTH MOTORCYCLE SPORTING ASSOCIATION

Standard Racing Regulations:

1. AGE GROUPS: Senior A (15½ to 17 years) — maximum engine capacity 125cc. Senior B (14 to 15½ years) — maximum engine capacity 125cc. Intermediate (11 to 13 years inclusive) — maximum

engine capacity 100cc. Junior (8 to 10 years inclusive) — maximum engine capacity 80cc. A rider who reaches the age limit agreed for classes on or after June 1 may complete the season in that class. Before his first event, a rider's birth certificate must be available for inspection by the secretary.

2. RIDING NUMBERS: Three plates will be carried, one facing forward at the front of the machine, one on each side of the rear of the machine facing outward. Minimum dimensions of the figures must be to A.C.U. Standing Regulations. Colours will be yellow plates with black numbers for Senior A, blue plates with white numbers for Senior B, green plates with white numbers for Intermediates, black plates with white numbers for Juniors.

3. MACHINES: Efficient silencers must be fitted at all times. Machines must be run on pump petrol (no dope). Throttles must be self-closing. Two efficient brakes must be fitted. Handlebar levers must be ball-ended or fitted with plastic covers. Handlebar ends must be filled in or covered. There must be no sharp edges on mudguards, silencers, footrests or frames. The whole machine must be safe and in good adjustment. Wheel sizes optional, but a rider must be able to touch the ground with both feet when seated normally astride his machine. Chain guards must be fitted to engine and wheel sprockets. No sleeved-down engines allowed.

4. CLOTHING: Crash helmets to be British Standard (i.e. Kite marked). Helmets and gloves to be worn when practising or racing. Goggles, if worn, must be of a splinterproof material. No tools or other hard objects may be carried in the pockets. Stout footwear of a satisfactory nature must be worn (Wellington boots not permitted). Clothing must not be allowed to flap and present a hazard to other riders.

5. GENERAL: Before practising, the machine and clothing must be presented to the scrutineer for examination in accordance with the regulations. A parent or guardian must be present at this examination, and sign on before the meeting. The scrutineer is empowered to exclude any rider whose machine or clothing is, in his opinion, not safe or in accordance with the regulations. One machine only may be ridden during any meeting, except in the case of genuine breakdown (when the use of a borrowed machine will be permitted).

6. FLAG SIGNALS: Union Jack — Start. Red — Stop. Yellow (held steady) — Caution, no overtaking until the hazard is passed. Yellow (waved) — Slow down to walking pace, no overtaking until the hazard is passed. Yellow with black diagonals — Last lap. Chequered — End of race or practice. Black (with a rider's number displayed, or indication to a particular rider) — That rider to draw off course.

7. PROTESTS: Any protests must be made on an official form, which can be obtained from the secretary or steward of the meeting. The protest

Andrew Arden's father organises schoolboy trials and scrambles in the East Midlands. He likes to see everything done in the correct manner, and his enthusiasm is infectious. This photo of 11-year-old Andrew was taken at a national schoolboy trial near Stoke Poges, Bucks, in 1975.

must be made on the day of the meeting, in order that it can be considered by the committee. Each protest must be accompanied by a fee of £1, which is returnable if the protest is upheld. Should a committee member be involved in a protest, he will stand down in order that a decision may be made. At least three committee members must be present for a protest to be considered.

8. ORGANISATION: Courses shall be marked in such a manner that no danger is presented to the riders. Spectator areas must be roped, and "prohibited area" notices displayed. First Aid personnel must be in attendance. Sponsoring of riders, or any form of advertising, will not be permitted unless authorised by the committee of the Y.M.S.A. Each organiser shall have the right to order the withdrawal of any competitor and/or machine which, in his opinion, constitutes a danger to other competitors. Riders who have competed in adult meetings shall lose schoolboy status.

KENT YOUTH GRASS-TRACK RIDERS ASSOCIATION

Racing Regulations:

1.   Riders will be divided into four groups, as follows: Class A — Between 7th and 10th birthdays. Machines up to 100cc (white/black numbers). Class B — Between 10th and 13th birthdays. Machines up to 150cc (blue/white numbers). Class C — Between 13th and 15th birthdays. Machines up to 200cc (yellow/black numbers). Class D — Between 15th and 17th birthdays. Machines up to 250cc (green/white numbers).

2.   The above groups will be determined by the age of a rider on January 1.

3.   Entry fee will be 50p per meeting.

4.   All entries, with money, must have been received no later than eight days prior to the meeting.

5.   Crash helmets are compulsory, and these must be to B.S.I. Standard 2001.

6.   Racing suits must be either leather or P.V.C. Body belts and back protectors are advisable.

7.   Riding boots must be zipped for easy removal.

8.   Gloves must offer full protection. Woollen gloves are not acceptable.

9.   Goggles, if worn, must not be glass-lensed.

10.   Engines are to be run on pump petrol only (no dope allowed). Petrol must be stored in metal cans, not plastic containers.

11.   Machines must be safely maintained, with no jagged edges and all moving mechanical parts covered. Machines will be examined before every meeting, and those not up to standard will be rejected.

12.   Machines must have brakes front and back, adequate chain guards, spring-back throttle, ball-ended handlebar levers, taped ends to footrests, and three number plates must be fitted. Only knobbly tyres may be used (no ribbed or bald tyres allowed).

13.   No rider will be allowed to participate unless he can touch the ground with both feet while normally seated astride the machine.

14.   Races will be of four laps each, with points scored four for 1st, three for 2nd, two for 3rd, one for all other finishers. A rider lapped once will receive one point regardless of finishing position, but anyone lapped more than once will receive no points. Anyone who rides outside the marker flags to gain an advantage will have one point deducted.

15.   No parents or riders allowed in the centre of the track whilst racing is in progress, without prior permission of the chairman or the clerk of the course.

16.   Riding of machines in paddock or other areas without permission of the paddock marshal will not be permitted.

17.   All parents and riders must sign in before

Older riders, such as Jamie Keir, have had the benefit of a good many years competing in schoolboy scrambles. They know the importance of regulations, and they realise that rules are compiled for the safety of the riders themselves. Mark rides mostly in Ringwood and Portsmouth events, and has a very professional approach to scrambling.

racing, after machine has been examined and passed.

18.   All riders must have knowledge of flag signals and act accordingly: Yellow — Caution, fallen rider (no change in race position until track is cleared). Black — Rider must pull into centre of track and stop. Red — All riders must stop immediately and return to start. Yellow with black diagonals — Last lap. Black and white chequered — Race finished.

19.   Members must ride in at least 50% of the K.Y.G.T.R.A. meetings from the time they join, to qualify for an End of Season trophy. Championship and Open meetings will count in that total.

20.   Riders who are not accompanied by their parents must bring a letter of authorisation signed by their parents.

21.   All protests, complaints and appeals shall be heard by the committee, whose decision will be final.

British Schoolboys Championship regulations are as per above, except for the following: Each boy will

Younger boys tend to disregard some of the regulations as being no more than needless complication and red tape. But all competitors have to abide by the rules, and this is in fact part of the training — part of the benefit to be derived from participation in schoolboy motorcycle sport. Here is little Mark Mellor, with no thoughts for anything but winning!

The Reading Schoolboy Scramble Club's rules formed a basis for several others. Here is Michael Watts, winning the intermediate contest in the Reading S.S.C. 10th anniversary scramble.

have no more than five rides in any meeting. Any boy who causes the stoppage of a race will be barred from the re-run except if the stoppage was due to the starting-tape being broken. Any boy ignoring the flag signals, or riding outside marker flags with both wheels (except for safety reasons), or receiving outside assistance after the 30-yard marker, will be excluded. Entry fee will be 75p per meeting. The top 16 riders on aggregate from all groups will qualify for the final.

SURREY SCHOOLBOY TRIALS CLUB

Trials Regulations (as per A.C.U. Youth Division, plus the following club rules):

1. Riders eligible to compete in S.S.T.C. trials shall be aged between 11 and 15 inclusive. On their 16th birthdays, members may stay on for a further year, but only competing for the 'Over 16' awards.

2. All new members join as novices. To become experts, they must win three awards (including one 'Best Novice' and two runner-up or first-class) in S.S.T.C. events.

3. Machine capacities as laid down in A.C.U. Youth Division regulations. Maximum capacity, 250cc.

4. Machines must be adequately silenced. They may be scrutineered at any time, and, if found faulty, will not be allowed to be used until the faults have been rectified.

5. No change of machine after trial has started.

6. Only trials tyres may be used (i.e., no 'knobblies').

7. Boots and crash helmets must be worn by competitors at all times while riding.

8. There shall be no riding prior to the start or during the lunch break.

9. Competitors must sign on and off, and return numbered bibs.

10. Novices will have easier observed sections than experts.

Crash helmets, gloves and leather boots are insisted upon by most clubs. Perry Leask favours the full gear — including helmet peak, goggles, face mask, shoulder pads and chest protector. He should know; he is one of England's most successful schoolboy scramblers.

Luckily for riders, there is no regulation which stipulates that work on the machines must be carried out only by the competitors! Chris Batt is grateful for the help provided by his father — here seen clawing lumps of mud off the bike in order to adjust the rear chain.

Paul Armstrong's father was a leading trials rider in Hampshire back in the 'fifties. Motorcycling is in the Armstrong blood, and young Paul takes the sport seriously. He knows the rules, he never argues with the observers when he is competing in a trial, and he looks forward to the day when he is old enough to ride in adult events.

Some clubs allow girls to ride — others restrict membership to boys. The Waltham Chase Boys M.C.C., despite its name, welcomes girls to take part in trials and display team work. Beverly Austen is this club's most successful girl member, and she is seen here on her 125cc Honda.

Schoolboy grass-track racing brings competitors together from all parts of the country. Here are Charlie Huxtable (Swansea) and Brian Canning (Canterbury) at the Kent Youth G.T.R.A. finals. For the benefit of all concerned, it is desirable that different clubs should operate under similar rules.

A couple of years ago, many schoolboy scrambles in the south were enlivened by very well-matched racing in the junior class between Kevin Tatum (304) and Philip Small (67). Here they are pictured at a Horsham S.S.C. event in Sussex — with Kevin holding a narrow lead.

11. Penalties in observed sections will be one mark for one touch, two marks for two touches, three marks for three or more touches, five marks for stopping or passing the wrong side of a section marker.

12. There shall be no riding two-up on machines during a trial.

13. Parents are expected to officiate as observers at trials.

14. Competitors must obey instructions at all times, in the interests of safety and continued use of land.

15. Regulations and results will only be sent to members who provide stamped and addressed envelopes.

16. Membership fee is £1.25 (which is made up of 75p membership and 50p joining fee). Badges are available at 30p.

HORSHAM SCHOOLBOY SCRAMBLE CLUB

Racing Rules:

1. On arrival, all machines must first be scrutineered by the machine examiner.

2. Entry fee must be paid for each rider, indemnification form signed by parent or guardian, and practice discs collected, before machines are allowed on the course for practice.

3. There shall be no riding off the marked course (unless a marked test area is provided) before or during the meeting. Disregard of this rule will entail exclusion from that day's meeting.

4. Any rider accidentally breaking the tapes and leaving the marked course shall rejoin the course where he left it. Anyone infringing this rule could be excluded from the meeting at the discretion of the competitions committee.

5. Machines shall be ridden at a walking pace in the pit area and up to the start line.

6. At all events, competitors will be under the control of the secretary. All complaints of a specific nature during the meeting should be made to the secretary. Complaints of a general nature should be made in writing.

7. So that all boys may have as many rides as possible, competitors should study the events board and be on the start line before the finish of the preceding race.

8. Engines of machines waiting on the line for the next race shall not be started until the last lap flag is shown for the race in progress.

9. There shall be no machine substitution for championship races.

10. No sponsored machines may be ridden at any Horsham Schoolboy Scramble Club meetings.

11. Members may join other clubs in order to obtain additional rides, but must support their own club meetings first.

All schoolboy scramble clubs have rules which stipulate what a rider must wear when competing. Certain minimum requirements are laid down, and no boy (or his parents) should be so foolish as to ignore these regulations. An A.C.U. jersey is favoured by Bob West — bearing the A.C.U. stamp of approval — along with leather boots, leather breeches, leather gloves, leather face-mask, goggles and a high-quality helmet. All very sensible.

Rob Doney is fully at home on all types of terrain — as happy going down as he is going up. Rob never scrambles or goes grass-tracking, he concentrates on trials organised by the Waltham Chase, Waterside and Surrey schoolboy clubs.

12. Crash helmets to a British standard (i.e., A.C.U. approved) shall be worn at all times.

13. Leathers (of bib and brace or waist type) shall be worn at all times. Jeans are not an acceptable substitute.

14. Jacket or jersey of strong material shall be worn, with full length sleeves. Sleeves must not be worn rolled up.

15. Leather boots to cover at least half the calf shall be worn at all times. Rubber boots are not an acceptable substitute.

16. Body belts are advised, and goggles (if worn) must be of splinter-proof material.

17. No hard objects shall be carried in pockets (e.g., tools, spares, plugs, etc.)

18. There are no restrictions on engine tuning.

19. Frames of any type are allowed, provided they are passed as safe by the scrutineer.

20. Handlebar levers must have ball ends.

21. Footrests must be of the folding type only.

22. Brakes must be efficient and safe.

23. Throttles must be self-closing (no tickover allowed).

24. Effective silencing devices must be fitted permanently.

25. Machines must have no sharp edges.

26. Standard petrol only may be used (as from petrol pumps).

27. Wheel sizes optional, but riders must be able to touch the ground with both feet when seated astride machine.

28. Tyres of any pattern except ribbed may be used.

29. Three number plates shall be firmly affixed to the machine, one facing forward on the front, one on each side at the rear. Minimum dimension of numerals is 5″ x ⅝″.

Schoolboy Motorcycle Clubs

Many adult motorcycle clubs have recently started Junior Sections which cater for schoolboys. They organise all forms of youth motorcycle sport, but most of the club activity is designed for adult members. With this in mind, the following list is confined to schoolboy motorcycle clubs.

Blackmore Vale Youth Motorcycle Club:
L. White, 110 Warminster Road, Westbury, Wilts.

Border Schoolboy Scramble Club:
Mrs. S. Churcher, 51 Bolle Road, Alton, Hants.

Bristol Grass Racing Combine Schoolboy Club:
S. Shortman, 61 Chipperfield Drive, Kingswood, Bristol.

Cambridge Juniors Scramble Club:
D. Dunn, 43 Edinburgh Road, Cambridge.

Carrickfergus Junior Motorcycle Club:
H. Smith, Smith's Car Sales, Whiteabbey, Newtownabbey, Co. Antrim.

Cornwall Schoolboy Scramble Club:
B. Annear, St. Blazey Service Station, Bridge Street, St. Blazey, Cornwall.

Corsham Schoolboy Scramble Club:
Mrs. A. Leyfield, "The Brendons", Corston, Malmesbury, Wilts.

Cotswold Schoolboy Scramble Club:
Mrs. L. Hill, 18 Glen Park Crescent, Kingscourt, Stroud, Glos.

Cotswold Youth Motorcycle Club:
R. Balster, 56 Newton Road, Hester's Way, Cheltenham, Glos.

Crowthorne Schoolboy Motorcycle Club:
Mrs. S. Birkett, 50 Wellington Road, Crowthorne, Berks.

Cumbria Youth Scrambles Club:
Miss A. Bardwell, 214 Yarlside Road, Barrow-in-Furness, Cumbria.

Devonport Schoolboy Scramble Club:
Mrs. J. Wenmoth, 23 Asbery Drive, Hooe, Plymouth.

Dragon Schoolboy Motorcycle Club:
D. Wainwright, 34 Colwyn Avenue, Rhos-on-Sea, Clwyd.

East Anglian Junior Scrambling Club:
G. Watton, 143 Rayleigh Road, Eastwood, Leigh-on-Sea, Essex.

Essex Junior Grass-Track Club:
V. T. Painter, 56 Longfield, Harlow, Middlesex.

Essex Schoolboy Trials Club:
Mrs. J. Towns, 13a Millers Close, Bocking, Braintree, Essex.

Horsham Schoolboy Scramble Club:
Mrs. S. Slight, 7 Cowdray Close, Pound Hill, Crawley, Sussex.

Kent Schoolboy Scramble Club:
J. Read, 6 Ladywood Road, Darenth, Dartford, Kent.

Kent Youth Grass-Track Riders Association:
Mrs. G. Luckhurst, Whitfield Hall, Beauxfield, Dover, Kent.

Kent Youth Motorcycle Club:
C. Golding, 36 Broxbourne Road, Orpington, Kent.

Kent Youth Trials Club:
B. Prior, 6 Beach Avenue, Birchington, Kent.

Lancashire Grass-Track Juniors:
Mrs. D. Newsham, 54 Elm Grove, Wigan Road, Leyland, Lancs.

Market Harborough Youth Motorcycle Club:
Mrs. S. Benson, 3 Tithe Road, Wood End, Wootton, Beds.

Medway Junior Motorcycle Club:
H. Hawkins, 35 Roebuck Road, Rochester, Kent.

Mid Antrim Junior Motorcycle Club:
J. Spence, 21 Ferniskey Road, Kells, Co. Antrim.

Midland Schoolboy Scramble Club:
Mrs. S. Baynham, "Baycott", Lawrence Lane, Cradley Heath, Warley, W. Midlands.

Mortimer & District Youth Motorcycle Club:
J. Challis, "Woodlands", King Street, Mortimer, Reading, Berks.

North Berks Youth Motorcycle Club:
Mrs. J. Beard, 45 Merritt Road, Didcot, Oxon.

North Devon Schoolboy Scramble Club:
C. Ireland, 50 Cornerways, South Street, Braunton, N. Devon.

Norfolk & Suffolk Junior Motorcycle Club:
Mrs. P. Bishop, Kettleborough Post Office, Framlingham, Woodbridge, Suffolk.

There were seven clubs in the British Schoolboy Motorcycle Association at the start of the last scrambles season, and each one was committed to organise a championship event — with points scored towards the B.S.M.A. championship titles. Here is a scene at the start of the first senior race at the fifth round in the 1975 series.

Some clubs, such as the Ringwood Schoolboy Scramble Club, organise trials in the winter and scrambles throughout the summer. Chris Adlem has for several years been one of the most skilful Ringwood club members, equally successful in trials and scrambles.

Norman Emery, from Durley, Hants, leads Terry Hayles and Andy Farr at a charity scramble near Petersfield last June. It was a good season for Norman, who emerged as one of the most successful members of the Portsmouth Schoolboy Scramble Club.

Nicholas Wraith, from Cheshire, was runner-up in the North-West Schoolboy Motorcycle Club's Junior Championships, 1973 and 1974. His father, Peter Wraith, was once a famous competitor and is now a member of the A.C.U. Youth Division committee.

Northern Ireland Junior Motorcycle Club:
Mrs. L. McBride, 22 Thornleigh, Ballydrain, Comber, Co. Down.

Northumbria Youth Scramble Club:
Mrs. W. Abbott, 32 North Magdalene, Medomsley, Consett, Co. Durham.

North-West Schoolboy Motorcycle Club:
J. C. Hopkins, "Craigmore", Handley Hill, Winsford, Cheshire.

Northern Youth Moto-Cross Club:
Mrs. V. Burns, 18 Mill Park, The Green, Millom, Cumbria.

Portsmouth Schoolboy Scramble Club:
E. Eltham, 27 Gudge Heath Lane, Fareham, Hants.

Reading Schoolboy Scramble Club:
Mrs. J. Bradbury, 564 Reading Road, Winnersh, Wokingham, Berks.

Rhayader Schoolboy Scramble Club:
T. W. Price, 23 Green Gardens, Rhayader, Powys.

Ringwood Schoolboy Scramble Club:
Mrs. E. Barrett, 3 Sunnyhill Road, Parkstone, Poole, Dorset.

Salisbury Youth Motorcycle Club:
K. Carter, 33 Coltsfoot Close, Amesbury, Wilts.

Sandwell Heathens Motorcycle Club:
P. Devall, 34 Regis Heath Road, Rowley Regis, Warley, West Midlands.

Severn Valley Schoolboy Scramble Club:
Mrs. E. Davis, 118 Langford Lane, Gloucester.

Sheppey Schoolboy Motorcycle Club:
P. Singleton, 76 Scooles Road, Minster, Sheppey, Kent.

Slough Ace Riders Club:
A. White, 5 Sherborne Drive, Windsor, Berks.

Somerset Schoolboy Scramble Club:
Mrs. E. Salter, 14 Mount Street, Bishops Lydiard, Taunton, Somerset.

Southampton Vikings Youth Motorcycle Club:
M. Hare, 93 Station Road, Netley Abbey, Southampton.

South-Eastern Grass-Track Juniors:
Mrs. L. Johns, 8 Risborough Drive, Worcester Park, Surrey.

South Humberside Youth Motorcycle Club:
R. Mills, 1 Orchard Close, Barton-on-Humber, South Humberside.

South Wales Schoolboy Scramble Club:
F. T. Dite, 35 Lakeside Drive, Cardiff.

South-West Junior Grass-Track Club:
Mrs. R. Major, 50 Church Road, West Huntspill, Highbridge, Somerset.

South-West Schoolboy Scramble Club:
Mrs. J. McMahon, Warley House, Warley, Totnes, South Devon.

Ted Hawker is chairman of the Waltham Chase Boys Motor Cycle Club, and a founder member of the A.C.U. Youth Division committee. Here he is seen giving advice to his son Jeremy at a junior trial in Hampshire last summer.

Stevenage Schoolboy Scramble Club:
J. Russell-Smith, 494 Rayners Lane, Pinner, Middlesex.

Surrey Schoolboy Trials Club:
Mrs. J. Dopson, Premier House, Farncombe, Goldaming, Surrey.

Torbay Schoolboy Scramble Club:
Mrs. R. Edwards, 136 Occombe Valley Road, Paignton, South Devon.

Waltham Chase Boys Motorcycle Club:
E. Simms, "Rosemary", Clubhouse Lane, Waltham Chase, Hants.

Warley Wasps Schoolboy Scramble Club:
R. Boxley, 38 Lapper Avenue, Lanesfield, Wolverhampton, West Midlands.

Waterlooville Youth Motorcycle Club:
B. Doney, Boarhunt Filling Station, North Boarhunt, Fareham, Hants.

Waterside Junior Motorcycle Club:
G. Swain, 9 Roberts Road, Hythe, near Southampton.

West Leeds Junior Motorcycle Club:
Mrs. B. Crowther, 18 Town Street, Gildersome, Leeds, West Yorks.

West Mercia Schoolboy Scramble Club:
Mrs. J. Skelding, 77 Market Street, Kingswinford, West Midlands.

York & District Youth Motorcycle Club:
R. Brigham, 117 East Parade, York.

Left

Sitting on the saddle, with both feet on the footrests and both wheels on the ground, is kid's stuff — according to Droxford lad John Taylor — a member of the Waltham Chase Boys M.C.C. display team. So John tries riding with his feet on the saddle and his front wheel high in the air — and he still steers a straight course!

A leading light in the schoolboy motorcycle club movement throughout the past ten years has been Bob Carpenter — a man who has perhaps done more than anyone else to bring the clubs together and to help patch up their differences.

As a tail-piece to this first book on the subject, Mr. Carpenter has a message to readers which contains some very sound advice. This is what he says:

'In spite of all the publicity which has been given to youth motorcycling, there are still many schoolboys who have no idea where their nearest club is based. With new schoolboy clubs being formed every few months, it is certainly difficult to keep track of them.

Although most clubs now have more or less standardised their age groups and engine capacities, it is foolhardy to rush out and buy a machine which you may find does not comply with club requirements.

So check with the club of your choice first concerning age and machine. You can usually join as many clubs as you wish, and the annual membership fees vary from £1 to £2. To compete can cost you anything from about 40p to 80p per meeting.

Don't believe that because you have ridden round a local field you will show everyone up when you join a club and start competing! Some youngsters perform like professionals and have learned from many years with schoolboy clubs.

It is no disgrace to finish last. Someone has to be there, and a good loser is always welcome! Remember, you must learn to walk before you can run, and never be afraid to watch how the really proficient lads ride — nor to ask their advice.

Every youth club official wants to help a beginner. This is what they are there for, so don't be afraid to join a club and become involved in the wonderful sport of schoolboy motorcycling. You will never regret it!'